"Them Days"

"Them Days"
Memories of a Prairie Valley

Olga Klimko
and
Michael Taft

FIFTH
HOUSE
PUBLISHERS

Cover design and art direction by John Luckhurst/GDL
Cover photograph by Richard Siemens

Printed and bound in Canada
93 94 95 96 97 / 5 4 3 2 1

The publisher gratefully acknowledges the assistance of the Saskatchewan Arts Board, The Canada Council, Communications Canada, and the Saskatchewan Heritage Foundation.

Canadian Cataloguing in Publication Data

Klimko, Olga

   "Them days" : memories of a prairie valley
   ISBN 1–895618–17–7

1. Souris River Valley - History. 2. Souris River Valley - Biography. 3. Frontier and pioneer life - Saskatchewan. 4. Saskatchewan - History - 1905–   *
I. Taft, Michael, 1947– . II. Title.

FC3545.S68K44 1993   97I.24'4   C93–098007–7
F1074.S67K44 1993

Fifth House Publishers
620 Duchess Street
Saskatoon, SK
S7K 0R1

Contents

Contents

Preface

The origins of "Them Days" can be traced back to an archaeological and oral history survey of Saskatchewan's Souris Valley conducted between 1984 and 1991 when the Rafferty-Alameda Dam complex was under construction. The purpose of the survey was to collect historical and archaeological data from the area before any changes occurred as a result of the building of the dam. The survey included the excavation of various ranches and farmsteads by archaeologists from Western Heritage Services, Incorporated; interviews of former valley residents by the authors; and the collection of photographs and memorabilia. We had no intention of publishing a book: the interviews were conducted only as background information for the archaeological work. But we soon realized that what we had here was far too valuable to be banished to some researcher's files or stored away in an archives. These memories belonged to the wider community, and everyone deserved to have access to them.

This book represents a departure from the manner in which most textbook histories are prepared. On the one hand it is a collaborative effort between archaeologists and oral historians, but it is also the result of cooperation between outsiders and local people. In essence, the people of the valley are the true historians, the real experts; we have merely collected and compiled the information they have shared so generously with us.

Acknowledgements

We could not have written this book without the help of many people. First and foremost, we would like to thank those who gave of their time to share their memories with us: Helen Blondeau, Norman Blondeau, Ernie Boyer, Jack Boyer, John Dowhanuik, Bella Gardipie, Uncle Ernie Hanna, Ernie and Esther Hanna, Carl and Margaret Hauglum, Marceline Lajimodiere, Arnold and Hazel Molstad, Jack and Joyce Muirhead, Gerald, Margaret, and Wayne Pick, Edgar Sawyer, and Clara Ziehl.

Many other people helped us by providing names of people to speak to and photographs. Our appreciation to: Paul Bachorcik, Louis and Otelia Beaulieu, Winnie Boyer, Rea Eagles, Matilda Eide, Fred Garneau, the Gilles family, Irene and Viola Halverson, Kathleen Hancock, Ben and Olive Hanson, Bill Hinzman, Ivan Horsman, John Johnson, Elmer and Lorne Kramer, Harold and Lila Longney, Gordon MacGregor, Karen Molstad, Roy Sanderson, Bev Sobush, Lloyd Sovdi, Clarence Steinke, and Sharon and Walt Stregger. We would especially like to thank Ruth and Roy McKague for their interest in the project and the valuable assistance they provided.

The staff of the Midale Museum were most helpful and cordial and allowed us access to their collection. At our camp on the Sandoff Ranch, the Sandoffs supported us in many ways and offered us their kind hospitality, for which we are very grateful.

The field staff, who braved ticks, heat, cold, and rain to map the historic sites and recover artifacts, deserve our thanks: Johanne Bédard, Monica Fraske, Miggs Greene, Joan Kanigan, Barbara Parr, and Dan Richert. For his work on the site, as well as his identification and documentation of the artifacts, we thank John Brandon, and our appreciation goes to Shelley McConnell for drafting the computer map. The staff of Western Heritage Services and its director, Jim Finnigan, provided technical expertise in the production of this book.

We would also like to acknowledge the Souris Basin Development Authority for financing our research. George Hood, former director of Planning and Operations at the Authority, gave us timely support and we thank him for it. Finally, our thanks go to the Saskatchewan Heritage Foundation for their financial contribution to the production of this book.

Dedicated to the people who settled the Souris Valley

Introduction

You will find here a collection of memories—memories roused from family photo albums; from things discovered buried in the ground; from old buildings, stone foundations, fence lines, and trees; from shrubs that mark (or marked) the landscape of this particular prairie valley; and from items preserved in people's homes and museums that recall the way of life of these early settlers. But most of all, this book is a collection of stories based on those memories, of "them days," when the Souris Valley was home to ranchers, farmers, and trappers.

The stories people tell about their lives rarely survive the tellers. Unlike photographs and artifacts, the oral history of a community remains alive only as long as there are people around who remember the old days. How often has someone remarked that they should have recorded an old settler on tape before he or she died? How often has an inquisitive outsider been told that "you should have been here when so-and-so was alive—she could have told you a lot about them days"? With each passing year, fewer old-timers remain, and there are fewer opportunities to record the history of a community in the words of those who are the keepers of the community's memories.

These pages capture a few of the memories of those who lived in and near the Souris Valley in Saskatchewan—but only a few, since the entire storehouse of recollections for any community would require volumes, rather than pages, and would be an ever-expanding collection as community members tell and retell, recall and revise, their memories of the old days.

This book, then, attempts to recapture the old days through people's memories, and to accompany those memories with photographs that evoke past times. The purpose here is not to record the facts of the valley's history, recount important events or people, or list the genealogies of the settlers—all worthy goals of most standard local histories. Instead, this is a collection of fleeting impressions and captured moments, of images frozen within the frames of photographs, and, more especially, in the memories of the people. The result is a kind of emotional history of the valley. For this reason, do not judge the book by its "facts"—different people have different memories and interpretations of "them days," and there is plenty of room for disagreement when the recollections of one person are compared with another's. Each resident of the valley has his or her own history, and each of these unofficial histories is as important as any official, factual history of the region.

How should you approach this history, then? Think of the times when you sat around with the old folks—maybe your own parents or grandparents—and listened to their reminiscences. Or think back to the times when you recalled your own past and shared those memories with family and friends. With the exception of a few passages from local books about the area, all of the recollections here are from tape-recorded conversations. We have not changed the words of the people, except to remove the "ums" and "ers" and the backtrackings of normal conversation. We have tried to remain as faithful to their actual words as possible, which means that the grammar of the stories might not be perfect, and you may run across the odd "expletive" here and there, added by the

speaker to spice up the reminiscence. But that's all right, for that is the way people talk, and this book contains the stories of the people, rather than the words of a historian. As you read these recollections, then, try to imagine the voices and to capture the flavour of the spoken word, so inadequately translated to the written page.

The people who contributed their memories and photographs to this book were all one-time residents of the Souris Valley or the land adjacent to the valley. They range in age from their fifties to nineties. Some have since died. Their backgrounds represent most of the groups that settled the valley: Métis, Scandinavian, German, British, American, and Ukrainian, but there were many other people from the valley who would have had as much or more to contribute to this oral history as those we interviewed. In this respect, our book should not be viewed as a final statement on the oral history of the valley, but as only a fragment of that history. There remain many stories to collect.

Settling in the Valley

The first settlers in the valley arrived from many different places. The area became home to English and Irish families from Ontario, Métis from North Dakota, Americans from the mid-western states, Scandinavians, Germans, Ukrainians, and other Europeans. But wherever they hailed from, they all faced the same challenges and hardships as they made a new life for themselves in the valley.

... early settlers

Ernie Hanna: I think my granddad and Uncle Ernie's dad—oh, I don't know if there was three or four brothers. I think they mainly come from Ireland in the early years. And they were up into Ontario or some place, you know— landed there first. And then moved south in 1904, in that period, to Iowa there, where they all homesteaded. There was just nothing, you know. There was just no feed or nothing. I guess they were just dried out. And they just left that country with covered wagons.

✦

Jack Muirhead: Oh, there was quite a few settlers in the valley. And in them days, there was people on every half or quarter, you know. And there was lots of wild land, too. A half-section was quite a bit of land, you know. That's the way they used to farm. They used to keep chickens and pigs. Cows—milk cows. Have a garden, and I guess they lived pretty rough, but like my mother said—she was ninety-two when she died—she said she never been cold and she never been hungry. So you know, they didn't have all the pleasures and the conveniences that we have, but they still had a good life.

✦

Jack Boyer: Our neighbour came here approximately at the same time as we did. I'm not sure. His father had a quarter right next to where we lived. He was just about eighty rods [440 yards] away from us, I guess. But we had a road allowance between us. And he lived there until he died in 1916. Yeah. And then my dad bought that quarter. And he accumulated a full section right then.

✦

Rose Boyer: On December 8, 1908, we arrived at Macoun but there was no

"Them Days"

Settlers arrived from many parts of the world to make a life for themselves in the Souris River Valley. The area became home to ranchers, farmers, trappers, and even the odd eccentric or two. *Courtesy Western Heritage Services, Saskatoon*

one to meet us. My husband, Louis, had gone to a dance the night before with Julius Venne. So we hired a three-seat Democrat buggy to take us all out to the farm. It was bitter cold but my daughter, Bella, was the only one who cried because she had cold feet. When we arrived at the farm everything was frozen in the house. Julius Venne was sleeping upstairs. Our cows were in the barn and when I tried to milk them for my children, they had no milk. Julius told me I could milk his cow but I told him I wouldn't have his cow here all the time and that my cows were fresh and I had to milk them. I pulled and pulled and finally got some milk. (excerpt from *Memories*)

✦

Jack Muirhead: 18 Highway, there's a plaque there. That's the sign of the first post office. I think my uncle Walter had the first post office there. And Grandpa, he homesteaded south of that. And I guess that was quite the life in those days, too. He came out and settled on the homestead, and then Grandma came—Mother was two years old, then—she was the oldest daughter—and they came out the next year. And they came by train as far as Moosomin, and then they came out by coach down the valley. There was no train line down there at the time. They came from Ontario. Now I'm not just

The Hannas, who established a ranch in the valley in 1912, were one of the first families to settle here. By today's standards, life was harsh and difficult for the early settlers. But old-timers seem as ready to reminisce about the pleasures of "them days" as they are about the hardships. *Courtesy Clara Ziehl, Midale*

sure of the area, but I know Mother said that when they first came out, the folks back home used to send them different things. And they helped them out quite a bit, when they first came out. I guess things were pretty tough. Grandma was a sort of a midwife and nurse—because they were ninety miles from a doctor at that time. So she did quite a bit of that in the neighbourhood. The Mounties used to patrol in those days on horseback. And she kept the Mountie there when he was in that part of the district. He would stay at their place.

Breaking the land was one of the first tasks of the early settlers, and their sons and daughters still tell stories of how neighbours cooperated to turn the valley into cropland.

◆

Edgar Sawyer: Our neighbour had a team of horses and he let the neighbours use them. At that time, they didn't have many teams. So they put a couple of outfits together, you see, and made one outfit out of them. And they would break with a little sulky plough, you know. Yeah. First year they broke up twenty acres. Of course, they farmed it then every year for quite a length of time before they would summer fallow.

◆

Jack Boyer: My dad told me that when he got this land, he hired somebody to break it up for him, and they were breaking with oxen. I don't remember seeing them at all, you know. I never did see oxen work, anyway. But I

Most settlers owned a quarter section of land. Unlike today, a half-section was considered a large farm. A good team of horses (or even a pair of oxen) was invaluable in the back-breaking task of turning the sod. *Courtesy Norman Blondeau, Macoun*

remember he told me that he had this old guy—I can't remember what the guy's name was—who broke the land for him and he used oxen.

✦

Carl Hauglum: Dad started off with two oxen and a horse. He worked on the railroad half the day, just halfways up to Halbrite here. There's a grove of trees by the highway yet. Dinnertimes, he'd walk over there to visit an old fellow. This fellow was madder than heck. He couldn't get his oxen to work. Hot, hot day. He was going to kill them and sell them. Dad said, "Don't do that. I'll take them. How much you want?" "Oh, you pay me when you get money," he says—the old bachelor that lived up there. Dad quit the railroad. He took off down to the south there to that

homestead. Broke it up with the oxen. Oh, he had trouble, too. If it was a hot day, they wouldn't work. They'd go to a slough and lay there till they got cooled off. Plough and everything went. He couldn't stop them. They're so powerful, you know. So he'd go early in the morning, or late in the evenings when it was cooler, and then they walk along slowly. They're not fast, you know. But strong, yeah, tough.

Margaret Hauglum: Well, they were probably trying to get away from the mosquitoes when they walked into the slough.

Carl Hauglum: Yeah, you had to leave them out there. When the flies or the

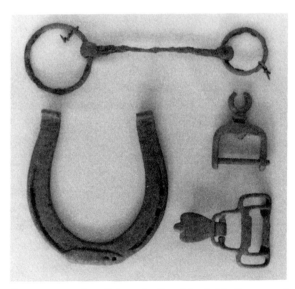

Horse gear such as this can be found buried in the ground of many old homesteads. Clockwise are a horseshoe, bit, harness trace, and harness fastener. Horseshoe from the Sawvell homestead (NE 1/4 18-5-12 W2), the remaining from Hinzman homestead (SW 1/4 7-3-9 W2). *Courtesy Western Heritage Services, Saskatoon*

mosquitoes were bad. They were tough then, too.

✦

Margaret Pick: Right in the valley there was just little fields. What Dad done was cattle mostly, and horses. I don't know when he started taking in herd cattle. Like community pasture. Now that was his whole life. He used to go around and gather up all the cattle all over—and horses—and then he'd chase them down in the valley and look after them for the summer.

Of course, the very first settlers were the Indians, and stories of how the "newcomers" and the Indians got along are still told by valley people.

✦

In later years, tractors would replace horses and oxen. *Courtesy Norman Blondeau, Macoun*

Jack Muirhead: But it was still pretty wild country, you know. The Indians were still more or less roving around. I know Mother said that her mother wasn't a bit afraid of the Indians. Like she said, the Indians, if you trusted them, you didn't have to worry. But if you didn't trust them, they'd steal everything. Oh, she said they'd come in—a whole tribe of them. Well, a tribe at that time wouldn't be that many, I guess. But they did travel in groups. And they'd come. They were curious and they'd come in the house and go through and they'd look at everything, but they wouldn't touch anything— curious to see how she lived, I guess. She said she'd sometimes wake up in the morning and there'd be a prairie chicken or duck on the floor. The Indians had been there and stayed the night and slept. And left this as a token that they were there. Just something to leave. And she said she thought the Indians were a very proud people, and she got along good with them. And that was just before the Rebellion, too.

The site (Sanderson site DhMs-12, NW 1/4 33-2-9 W2) at which these Indian artifacts were found was occupied from 1000 A.D. until 1700 A.D. Native people, of course, had lived on the land long before white settlers arrived. Bone spatula at the top; middle from left to right—stone knife, scraper, stone arrowhead, rim of a pot; bottom from left to right—bone bead, metal arrowhead, metal cone clothing ornament. *Courtesy Western Heritage Services, Saskatoon*

There was no trouble in that area. Only trouble they had was the bloody American cowboys would come over and steal their horses. Yeah, I heard that before from different ones. They'd wait till Sunday, you know, when everybody was in church, and then come and steal their horses. Horses in those days were worth a lot of money.

A good team of horses would bring five or six hundred dollars, and that was real dollars in those days, you know, when you worked for a dollar a day. And five or six hundred dollars meant quite a bit. It couldn't be more than twelve or fifteen miles from the border, I suppose. Here in Estevan it's nine. And those days it was wide-open country. And it wouldn't be hard to go down the Souris River and drive a bunch of horses down into the States. Once they got across the line, I guess they figured they were home free.

But there's a story that Mother used to tell about. These people, they were horse ranchers in the valley. And one of them come in one evening and said that their horses were gone. Somebody had taken their horses. And he grabbed his rifle and a pack, and put some food in the back of his saddle, I suppose. Away he went. And he come back about three days later, and he had his horses. And apparently these cowboys had come over and stole the horses, and he tracked them. And he caught up to them and apparently shot them. He didn't fool around. I suppose he crept up on them at night and shot them, and got his horses and come back. And that was it.

◆

John Dowhanuik: And when we first homesteaded there in 1916, there was Indians. I don't know where they come from or where they went. But they would stop in to our place every once in a while. They wanted handouts. So Mother would give them a loaf of bread or something. And they rode horses, and they went west. Where they come from, nobody knew.

The valley was a lonely place for some of the new settlers—especially women. Some settlers adjusted to valley life, while others moved on, but all newcomers faced the challenge of adapting to a very different way of life.

◆

Carl Hauglum: My mother wouldn't live down there in the valley. She just got married—miles from neighbours and no road. Coyotes howling. Left alone, scared at night. They'd be howling early in the morning. She didn't want to live there. Dad had to move. Most of them come from a country where there were a lot of people. Minnesota—that's where she come from. Neighbours all over, knew everybody. But on the prairies—four or five miles and there's not a soul around. Come wintertime, you see, you couldn't go out—no road to go by to find home. That was one thing she was worried about. And I was just born out there, too. She didn't want to leave me out there all by myself—her and me—lonely carrying a baby. So she suggested to Dad that they take off and move closer to neighbours.

◆

Carl Hauglum: I didn't know a word of English when I started school. Not one

word. Well, a lot of them around here were the same. The parents couldn't talk a good English. We taught the parents English—the kids, you know. I remember Henry, a neighbour's boy— he was two years ahead of me. I sat at the desk and the teacher was talking to me, and I looked and looked—"What you talking about?" She knew Henry— he was Norwegian, too. And he had to translate to me across the desk. They finally set me in the same desk as Henry. They had two people at the same desk in these old schools. Remember that? Two together. So they could talk. Henry translated every word the teacher told me. It was rough. A lot of people were like that.

Margaret Hauglum: Kind of hard to learn that way.

Carl Hauglum: The first year or two we had to learn the language.

. . . building a homestead

Along with breaking the land, the most important task for the settlers was building a home and farm buildings. Sometimes the settler's first house was a rather temporary structure—a sod house or a dugout.

◆

John Dowhanuik: The house was just wood and mud—an old-time mud house. When my dad built the house, it was made out of mud.

◆

Edgar Sawyer: Our first house. It was

The homesteader's cookstove served to cook the meals and heat the house, and satisfying the need for fuel was a never-ending job. All that is left of this cookstove from the Hinzman homestead (SW 1/4 7-3-9 W2) are these pieces. This family lived relatively close to Estevan and likely travelled there to purchase their coal. Many other families in the area resorted to digging for their own coal. *Courtesy Western Heritage Services, Saskatoon*

just shacks, you know. And Dad would build onto it. Maybe a bedroom or something on it. Well, I was born in it.

✦

Uncle Ernie Hanna*: We had a heater and a cookstove in the house—two stoves. I tell you right now, it was kept warm—but that's it. The house had two bedrooms upstairs, one bedroom downstairs, and a sitting room. And a lean-to on the side for a kitchen and for going down in the cellar. It had a cellar underneath it.

✦

Helen Blondeau: Well, the first house we lived in, it was just a one-room house,

maybe about as big as these two rooms in my house now. And then there was an upstairs with two rooms in it. To us, it was roomy, I guess, because we didn't know the difference. It was a real warm house. It was a high house and it was warm. Oh, we never suffered in the wintertime. We used to have real cold winters years ago—colder than what they are now. There was two bedrooms upstairs. My mother and dad had one bedroom and some of the kids had one bedroom, and then some slept downstairs on a cot.

✦

Ernie Hanna: The two bedrooms on one side was never that cold, no. But my sisters slept in the furthest one back, you see. The coldest one. They'd pee in a pot and it would freeze, you know.

---

* "Uncle" Ernie is the older of the two Ernie Hannas interviewed.

And the old toilet was just up from the house. You know, we had outdoor bathrooms.

✦

Clara Ziehl: Well, it wasn't much of a house. But I thought it was quite a house then, you know. There was a kitchen and a living room and a dining room. I think there was three bedrooms. There was quite a family of us, you know. But we all slept in the three bedrooms. Then there was a veranda, too.

✦

Ernie Hanna: There were just three rooms: the dining room and then the front room and the folk's bedroom in the corner. And then there was kind of a little bit of a jog in there, and that was all veranda, closed in with a screen.

A cobblestone foundation and a cellar hole are all that remain in this spot now, but at one time a prefab house purchased from Eaton's and delivered by train stood on the Muirhead farm. *Courtesy Jack and Joyce Muirhead, Estevan*

A number of different families and single men lived on the CPR water pump house homestead at various times, each adding buildings or making changes to suit their own particular needs. This photo was taken in 1943, when the Boyer family lived here. The main house can be seen on the right, with the various outbuildings to the left. *Courtesy Helen Blondeau, Midale*

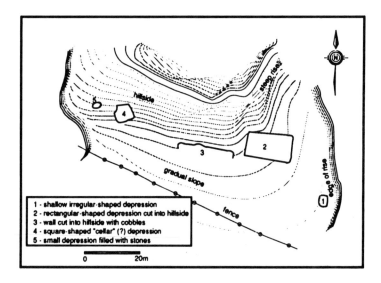

1 - shallow irregular-shaped depression
2 - rectangular-shaped depression cut into hillside
3 - wall cut into hillside with cobbles
4 - square-shaped "cellar" (?) depression
5 - small depression filled with stones

This computer-drafted map depicts the various features found on an abandoned homestead in the valley (possibly the Lord homestead) by the archaeological team. These sites and the memories of the former residents are virtually all that remain of a way of life that has practically disappeared. *Courtesy Shelley McConnell, Western Heritage Services, Saskatoon*

John Dowhanuik: Our house was about fourteen feet wide and maybe twenty feet long—something like that. Just two rooms. One room was the kitchen and the other was the front room. That's where we lived, where we all grew up. Eight kids in there. In the front room, we had about three beds in there and had a stove—a heater—and in the kitchen part there, we had a cook stove and a cupboard. We ate in the front room. Some slept on the floor and some on the beds, wherever there was room.

Hazel Molstad: The rooms? There wasn't any. One room downstairs and one upstairs. We had it partitioned off— we put a curtain between the beds.

Margaret Pick: Mattresses, we packed straw in. I can remember straw mattresses. And when they got dirty, you'd take it out and pack clean straw in it. You'd go to bed and it would crunch until it got packed down.

Helen Blondeau: Our second house was the old CPR pump station house. It had a wood floor, but the stone walls were cold, and they had those big windows, those big bay windows. So it was a nice-looking house outside, but it sure was cold in the wintertime.

Ernie Boyer: There was sort of a hole there where you had the barn. Half of it was in the hill and the other half was

The depression seen here (feature #2 on map opposite) was used as a barn and storage area. A hole was dug into the hillside so that earth formed three of the walls, and a roof was added, as described by Carl Hauglum (below). The building then served to house animals, store hay, etc. *Courtesy Western Heritage Services, Saskatoon*

roof. It wasn't all completely open— part of it was in the hill, you see. There was a lot of those barns that way in those days. The front was built with lumber—just the front. The back part, where it was in the ground, they didn't use no lumber or nothing. That's why they built them that way. And a lot of them had a sloping roof with shingles and lumber, but some were built just with dirt and thatched roof.

✦

Gerald Loring Boyer: We had a very old barn built into the side of the hill with a roof made of poles and straw bales. I remember how on winter nights I would go up with Dad when he milked

the cows. On one occasion just before Christmas, I had apparently been told stories of how baby Jesus was born in a manger, and I imagined that it must have looked just like our old barn. Every Christmas I remember it again. (excerpt from *Memories*)

✦

Carl Hauglum: The very first barn—that was a one-storey with one small up-stairs part on it, and a lean-to. Didn't have much of a barn then. Nobody had good barns in the early days, you know. Didn't have money. Some barns didn't have siding. Straw on top for a roof. A pile of timbers with a pile of straw laid on top. Some of them had a slope. No, nobody had big barns in them days. Shacks or sheds, they called them. Wasn't too much. No roof. Lot of them had poles across the top and piled straw or hay on top to keep the winter weather out.

✦

Ernie Hanna: Well, we generally always had the barn pretty well full. I don't know how come. Well, it would just be the late colts in the fall, and some that would get distemper, or something, you know, that needed special care. They couldn't just go out on their own. And that was the same with the cattle. We used to feed some of them on one side of the barn—we had these single stalls. And the other side was double stalls. I guess about four or five double stalls on the south side. And on the other side,

This storage shed, built into the side of a hill, is used today at the Sandoff Ranch. Note how the roof is level with the ground surface. The building looks like part of the hillside if approached from behind. *Courtesy Western Heritage Services, Saskatoon*

five or six or seven. We'd just keep the livestock in there and water them. Never even turn them out. Feed them before shipping them out, or during the winter, so they'd be fatter for butchering.

We built our fences with posts about eight inches apart, and then mostly willows or small trees—willows mainly. You'd just cut them and just keep laying them in. And then every little ways, you'd tie them together with wire so they couldn't pull apart, and they would settle down together. And so you had about an eight-inch wall of just brush, you know. And then we had made fancy pole gates. We had

them braced and we had a band around the top—an iron band on the post coming down. We braced it with a plank, so you'd catch a hold of the little thing and swing it around—kind of a pin in the ground, and the bottom of the plank went up into the centre of the post to hold the bottom in place.

We also had a "sheep fence," as we called it at that time—kind of an old wire with a barbed wire on top, I would say. Quite a high fence. And then up from our hospital barn we had a shed. And then the cow barn. There was room for twenty-four head there. And then we had another place where you could pile feed and stuff in between them two buildings. So we could carry the feed in and could just throw it over the fence. The corral went right from by the cow-barn door. And then we had another one of them gates in the middle, and then another big corral out behind. Yeah. And then right out on the outer side end, we had just a round brush corral about thirty feet across, a round one. There was a snub post in the centre, and on the outside edge we had a chute for branding cattle. Used for rodeos, mostly. You could chase them in there and when you opened the gate in the front, why they were going. And that's where they had the rodeos, in there.

And yeah, I can remember now, too, having a tie corral. You dig a ditch two or three feet deep—a trench—and then stand railroad ties on end in there, and nail a board or something on each side to hold them in place. A tie corral, yeah. Dug a trench maybe pretty near a foot wide, and you'd stand the ties on end in there tight, one against the other. And then strike a plank or board or something onto them—one on each side—to hold them, and put the dirt back in around them.

Wood was scarce in the valley. The small trees that grew along the river, even when used, didn't make the best building material, but if settlers wanted to buy the lumber shipped to the yards in Macoun, Halbrite, and Estevan, they needed cash. The result was that people tended to reuse old houses, barns, and even fences, either moving whole buildings onto their property, or tearing them down and reusing the wood for other structures.

Because of the shortage of wood in the valley, wooden buildings were seldom left to sit and rot, even in recent times. This old house was moved from the Boyer homestead and was still being used during the 1980s on the Gilles farm for hay storage. Pigs were kept underneath the house, on the left side. *Courtesy Western Heritage Services, Saskatoon*

Arnold Molstad: Reusing buildings and fences was done a lot. If you wanted to extend a building, you'd just take out a wall and build from there. I think I ended up with my grandfather's house in the end. I built a garage out of it, until it fell down. And like a fence—you wouldn't think of running to town and getting new lumber. If there was a fence your neighbour didn't want any more, you'd try and buy it from him.

✦

Edgar Sawyer: Well, there was some of our old house out there we used for a chicken barn, and some of it the neighbour come and bought—what we called the dining room. And he moved that down to his place. That was Albert Lajimodiere. He moved that down to a quarter he had down south. And it was there for a long, long time. Then when he moved to Estevan, right beside Galloways—across from Galloways— he had a little forty acres or something down there. He moved it down there. And what happened to it after? Maybe it's going yet. I don't know.

✦

Ernie Boyer: John Lord's abandoned house was still there when I was six or seven years old. And we bought the house from the person that owned it and hauled it to our place and added it to the other house we had. So that was part of our buildings. That one was just added to the main house.

✦

Ernie Hanna: I bought a neighbour's house and moved it in—started to move it in. Going to put it on a basement up here. I got as far as Elswick, I guess, and decided to sell it to my wife's brother. Now it's setting down here in town, two blocks down east, right at the corner. And we put a floor on our basement and lived in the basement with a floor on it, that winter.

I helped move a neighbour's house. I remember, that was when the first community pasture was started. I guess he bought land right over straight south of Goodwater, and then we moved a house from there over to his other land. And it was just a narrow, high, two-storey house. Man, it was heavy. Plaster in between the two-by-fours and then on the outside again. I had it loaded on timbers and old steel-wheels—separator wheels, maybe. And I had that old Chevy—three-ton Chevy. I remember we broke an axle just when we was going to pull out with it, and the bolts kept coming loose. I had it welded in. I had a heck of a job getting that chiselled apart, so you could get the axle out and put a new one in. I think I had to buy a new hub that time to fix it. But I can remember when we started to move her across, we had to go—oh, I don't know—maybe three-quarters of a mile or something—kind of across the pasture—and angle it to the other road. And we started across there, and we stopped to take the fence down and see about getting onto the road again. And we was over, opening the fence up, and this man's wife, she hollered out, "Dinner's ready!" On the old coal stove, she'd cooked dinner—a good big dinner for us right while we was going across that rough ground. I could never get over it.

✦

Jack Muirhead: We did get help from the VLA [Veterans Land Administration] to build the house. And then I got a chance to buy this big barn. The barn was 110 feet by—well, it had thirty-two feet in the centre and then two leans the full length. Sixteen-foot leans on it, the full length of the barn. A big, big barn. I got that for one thousand dollars. So I hired a crew and I had my brother as a kind of a foreman, and we tore the bottom out. And we saved— what?—eighteen feet. A big loft, a huge loft. And then they cut it in two. A guy went with a hand saw, up one side and down the other. And the lean-tos— well, of course we took the roof off the lean-tos. And then we cut the walls in sixteen-foot lengths, and hauled them home. In sixteen-foot lengths. And the other part, they hauled it home. And then I had two big hay barns. And so I put the loft on five-foot stubbings, and we tied it in. The barn was tied in— every rafter was double tied in. Just a beautiful building. And we tied it in to this stubbing, and bolted it onto a cement foundation. And then we had planks around the outside, and left an opening, so the cows could eat. And we blew feed into the barns. Filled them up. Just a heck of a good way to feed cattle.

✦

Ernie Hanna: That hospital barn, it just had a peaked roof. It was all built out of old lumber, pretty much. Yeah, and that cow barn—I should remember that. Because they'd just hauled it home in long slabs. They just took it apart and got a wagon right alongside of it, with poles on it, and tipped it over onto it, and all fastened on, and hauled her home. And then they just laid it down, kind of, so that they were ready to stand it up, and put it together again, rather than tear it down.

. . . clothes

Like wood, clothes were also reusable. Settlers received hand-me-downs from relatives in the East, ordered clothes from the mail-order catalogue, or made their own. In the old tradition of not allowing anything to go to waste, people never threw away clothing that could be patched, incorporated into another piece of clothing (or quilt), or at least used for cleaning rags.

✦

Margaret Pick: My mom's sister had one child, and they had money. And three or four times a year, we'd get a great big box from them, and that was a lot of the clothes we wore.

Helen Blondeau stands in front of the CPR water pump station homestead where her family lived for a time. The new coat she is wearing was probably ordered through the Eaton's catalogue. *Courtesy Norman Blondeau, Macoun*

✦

Helen Blondeau: Well, we'd send for clothes from Eaton's. I remember my mother used to make big orders for Eaton's in the spring. She'd make big orders. I guess the clothes were cheap. And then sometimes they'd go to the States and buy some cheap cotton.

✦

Jack Muirhead: She made the kids' clothes. By golly, Joyce was good at making them. She was too tight to even buy a pattern. She looked in the catalogue and take a piece of paper—

Joyce Muirhead: Would you please explain that I didn't have twenty-five cents to buy a pattern? That's what patterns were worth at that time. All I did was get the Eaton's catalogue, and look in there to see what I wanted to make, and made it. And I never did have a pattern. Somebody would give me some clothes or something, and I would rip them all up and turn them inside out, you know, because the bright side was on the underside. And the material was really good, and I cut patterns out of newspapers, till I got the right size for whatever kids I was making clothes for. And myself. I made all my own clothes—I still do. And that way I don't need a pattern, all I need is a picture.

Jack Muirhead: Even made our coats. Yeah, she used to make their coats, even. I had an old army great coat that she made, oh, a dandy coat out of that, and all the kids in Hitchcock wanted her to make one for them, too.

... cures

Just as most buildings and clothes were homemade, the settlers relied on their own medical knowledge to treat their various ills. There were few if any doctors in the area, and of course not all settlers could afford the services of a doctor. For the most part, doctors were a last resort, when home remedies no longer worked.

Arnold Molstad: Most curing was done in the home, you know. But we had to go to town to just get some medicine. But it wasn't like now. We bought mostly liniment, aspirins.

✦

Clara Ziehl: Well, we used very few medicines in them days. Castor oil, we used mainly.

✦

Edgar Sawyer: Oh, they rubbed your chest with goose lard. Yeah, that's supposed to take out the soreness and loosen up the cold. And then you soak your feet in hot water. And mustard, oh God—sulphur—pretty potent stuff, that sulphur.

✦

Margaret Hauglum: Goose grease for colds. And what else? They used to put a drop of coal oil on sugar for coughs, didn't they?

Carl Hauglum: They had a lot of remedies back in them days.

Margaret Hauglum: Bread and milk poultices for infections.

Carl Hauglum: Flax—they used flax poultices. What was that for?

Margaret Hauglum: That's for infections, too.

Carl Hauglum: Sulphur and mustard, wasn't it?

Margaret Hauglum: Sulphur and molasses.

Carl Hauglum: For flu or lungs.

Margaret Hauglum: In the spring if you needed some iron to give you some pep,
well, they'd give you sulphur and molasses. If you get something in your eye, put a flax seed in your eye.

Carl Hauglum: Yeah, put a flax seed in to clear your eye out. Did you ever hear of that? It's so small it floats, you see.

Margaret Hauglum: You just drop the flax seed in your eye, and in the morning the flax seed and the dirt will be in the corner.

Carl Hauglum: Yeah, if you get dirt in your eye, it brings it out. Because flax is smooth and slicky, too, you see. You don't soak it or anything. It will float around. There's a lot of remedies they had them days.

Margaret Hauglum: Mustard plasters, good for colds and chest colds.

Carl Hauglum: Burn your chest awful to have that sulphur pad or mustard pad on. Put it in a sack, you see, and lay it on. It's for pneumonia or a bad case of cold. You get red there on the chest where you leave it on so long. About an hour or a half-hour, was it?

Margaret Hauglum: And there was lots of midwives around.

Carl Hauglum: A lot of them. There's a lot of home nurses, too. Lot of them did their own. There wasn't no one in town. Too far to get a nurse and too costly to get them.

✦

Helen Blondeau: We used to pick out different flowers, wild flowers, to make cough medicine. They were some kind of little yellow flowers. I remember; I don't think they have any around here.

They used to be down in the valley. We'd pick these little flowers and boil them, and that was good for cough medicine. I wouldn't know what kind of flowers they were—or weeds, whatever they were. Must have been weeds.

◆

John Dowhanuik: Martin. He was a doctor of some kind. He'd try to heal you, you know. One guy had trouble with his hand—from the mines. He hurt his hand and it wouldn't heal up. So Dr. Martin gave him some roots and stuff and water, and he put that on his hand. And in a few weeks it healed up.

◆

Carl Hauglum: Like old Molstad out there. He was kind of a pretty good vet, a local vet that worked for everybody. He loved that work, and he loved animals. He lived in the river hills there, too.

◆

Hazel Molstad: Your dad was able to fix horses, too.

Arnold Molstad: Yeah, he was a veterinary. He was on the road all the time. Oh yeah, fixed horses' teeth, colic, and get the calves born from cows.

. . . neighbours, characters, and travellers

Out of the individual settlements in the valley grew a sense of community. After a few years, the farmers and the ranchers, whatever their backgrounds, began to see themselves as "valley people." Some of the most interesting stories about the early years in the area relate to the people themselves: good neighbours, local characters, or those who simply travelled through.

◆

Gerald Pick: Uncle Ernie had an agreement with a fellow to break I-forget-how-many saddle horses. And he said, "I would have had money enough out of that to buy a farm." So he was out in the hills. He chased these things in the corral, and he had five or six of them broke when word come out that this guy died of a heart attack and was in debt up to his neck. And his wife was in bed with arthritis. So Ernie went up there and said to the man's wife, "What are you going to do?" Well, she didn't know. Well, Ernie said, "I told her, now you keep still. You don't even know me, till you see me again." And he says, "I went back out where nobody—bankers or nothing else—knew where I was, and I grabbed these"—and there was six or eight horses. He said, "I went around to the ranchers. They were all pretty obliging. I got seventy-five or eighty dollars a head for them. I collected a bundle of money and went up back there, and the widow says, 'What do I owe you?'" Ernie says, "You don't owe me nothing. Goodbye." And he said that he remembered she had a son that went up in northern B.C. some place. And then a fellow named Gordon from Midale that was up in that country went down to Midale, and Ernie asked him, he said, "Did you ever know anybody up there?"—I forget the name now. "No," Gordon said, "but I can look around when I get home. Why?" Ernie said, "Well, I'm just kind of interested in where this young fellow"—she had a son—"ever got to." And I'll be damned if about two weeks after Gordon went home, he found this kid's name in a phone book and he phoned him and he told him Ernie Hanna was asking about him. So Ernie gets a letter from this young guy, and he wrote, "You old goat, you. You never come out to see me, and I'm coming to Midale to see you." And he came all the way to Midale to see Ernie.

There were a few local characters in the valley—personalities who are still recalled by valley people because of their peculiar ways. George Faggetter was probably the best known of these eccentrics, and even if people no longer remember his name, they still remember the old bachelor who built his houses in stone, who never worked for money, and who studied religion.

✦

Jack Boyer: There was an old bachelor that's long gone. He was another old bachelor that lived south of us here. He had an old shack built with stone right in the hill. Kind of an old dugout. Had a roof on, dirt floor. I don't know how he survived.

✦

Ernie Boyer: I remember lots of times

The valley had its share of characters and eccentrics. George Faggetter was probably the most well-known local to fit that description. He was born in Oxford County, England, in 1858, where he learned the trade of stone mason. George refused to handle money, built his dwellings out of stone, and was extremely self-sufficient. The remains of these two or three buildings, which were on the site of his first home, can be seen from quite a distance away. *Courtesy Western Heritage Services, Saskatoon*

visiting George Faggetter. He was self-sustaining. I don't know how he could do it, but the only thing that he got from outside was what people give him. He wouldn't buy and he wouldn't sell. I don't know how he existed. I still remember, he was quite a good talker, and he was an Englishman. He was real English. He come from England. He was well educated. I wish I had some of his writing—what he used to write about. You'd be surprised how nice he would write. Anything he had, he made it himself—everything. He was as self-sustaining as he could be. He would never buy nothing, he would never take money, no. So when you hired him, you had to pay him with food, shoes. Faggetter built the stone buildings for the CPR pump station. That's when they found out he wouldn't take money. The CPR wanted to pay him money. So somebody else took the money that they were supposed to give to Faggetter and he'd get his shoes and stuff from those people. Faggetter wouldn't handle that money.

✦

Helen Blondeau: Oh yeah. When we were real young, George Faggetter used to live right across the river from us in a little coolie. And he had built a stone house himself. They said he was a stone mason. Yeah, and he built his own house. Oh well, I remember us kids, we used to go and visit him when we were quite small. And he'd read the Bible to us. So he must have been religious. And he was quite a hermit. I mean he was a real hermit, I always said, because you'd read about hermits and he sure must have been a hermit, because he wouldn't take money for anything. And he'd make his own flour with wheat. He'd grind it himself. And he'd go fishing to eat. And then he'd come and work for Dad, and Dad would give him certain food to eat. Because he wouldn't take money. He'd eat a lot of berries and stuff. And I know he'd eat a lot of fish, because he'd be fishing every day. So he must have nearly lived on fish.

✦

John Dowhanuik: George Faggetter—he was one of these guys who didn't believe in money. He lived in about three places. First place he lived was on the south side of the Macoun dam. But the thing was, the municipality wanted him to pay taxes, and he didn't believe in money. So he moved out of there, and he built another shack west of Art Jones. We used to go to school and go by his shack. And then he built another shack in a coolie, and he built it right on the correction line. He said, "That land didn't belong to nobody." So that's where he built his shack, and that's where he stayed. He was the kind of a guy who always predicted the future. When people would come down to the valley to pick berries, George Faggetter would entertain them with a kind of church service—on Sunday to a bunch of people. He'd try to preach the future. And everybody listened to him.

George Faggetter seated outside of his last home, a tiny 6 x 10 x 7 1/2 foot shack made from stone and dirt. People seemed to accept his different way of looking at the world and admired him for his independence (what he could not earn, make, pick, or grow for himself, he bartered for) and obvious intelligence. *Photo taken by Axel Vinge, courtesy Viola Halvorson, Torquay*

Arnold Molstad: Some guys from Estevan came out and wrecked all his Bible work.

Hazel Molstad: He rewrit the Bible many times. He'd come up and he'd have a pack of papers like that.

Arnold Molstad: He was quite a friend of Hazel's folks.

Hazel Molstad: He'd have no way to go except walk. I remember one time, he came along with his wheelbarrow full of fish. He'd come early enough so it wouldn't be too hot. You couldn't pay him anything, but we'd give him a loaf of bread or whatever. Bake him a pie.

Arnold Molstad: Oh, he was religious all the time. He could sing like a bird. That's what Dad said. And he played the piano.

✦

Marceline Lajimodiere: Our barn was

kind of on a side hill. The water used to run down into the barn on the floor. That's when Mr. Faggetter come in and put in the stone floor. That floor is there yet, now, sure, because nobody ever moved them stones. It was Mr. Faggetter done that work. And we used to go and bring food for him. He wouldn't accept money. We used to bring him meat and stuff like that, whenever they butcher in December.

✦

Jack Boyer: Well, old Faggetter, he was digging coal where he lived and getting coal in that area. I don't know how good it was. It couldn't have been very good coal. Lignite coal.

✦

Edgar Sawyer: Yeah, he lived like a

badger. While he was building the stone house, he just dug a hole in the side of the hill. Squirrels used to come in and have dinner with him.

◆

Jack Boyer: Well, it's a funny thing with him. I don't know how he lived. Of course he depended on his neighbours feeding him quite a bit. But he'd eat berries or any damn thing that he could find, just like a goat. He used to eat fish, too. He was kind of a religious man. I don't know—but he didn't want anything to do with the government at all. I sure laughed when he told me one time when he was living in that last place he lived—in the valley and the creek that he moved to—in the wintertime a weasel came in to live with him. And he said he was kind of scared of her, but she stayed with him all winter. Well, it's unbelievable. Can you imagine a wild animal bunking in with you, especially a weasel?

There were other characters to rival George Faggetter. Some, like Pete Baker, were not actually from the valley, but everyone in the valley knew them.

◆

Margaret Pick: And of course you've heard of old Pete Baker. He came to town and nobody I don't think ever knew where he come from or what he was or anything. He never worked. He was the town's handyman. And I think the town paid him a little and he would keep every scrap of paper and everything. And he never bathed and never changed his clothes. But if he got a new pair of pants, they went on over the top of the old. He was a little tiny guy. He'd fold the cuffs up several times, one over the other. And I can remember—on the street—that he'd never pass you—when we were kids, I suppose—that he wouldn't take your hand like this and he'd stick a nickel in it. And oh, we'd be so tickled. We'd go in to buy something with that nickel. They finally give him a room in the hotel.

Gerald Pick: And you go and talk to any of the old farmers around here—that man had a mind like nobody! Guys would be coming in and buying parts, and old Pete had to talk to everybody and ask them why they come to town. But they come for this—"Well, why do you want to go and buy that for? You got one laying in your yard." And he'd tell them where it was laying in their backyard. Now he just kind of memorized just what everybody had.

Margaret Pick: And he yelled. He never spoke normally. He screamed, you know. And you could hear him all over Main Street when he was talking.

Gerald Pick: Of course all the older farmers, now they're dead, but I know they've often talked about the money old Pete saved them, because he knew more what was in their junk piles than they did, and he'd send them back home.

Another character was that old John Klyne.

Margaret Pick: He remembers.

Gerald Pick: Ralph Blondeau—was always telling the story about old John. "Just when my horse got to liking sawdust, he died."

✦

Jack Boyer: One old character—Hobert—he was an Englishman. Yes, he was a servant of the Queen at one time. His wife was, too. They're both dead quite a few years.

✦

Jack Muirhead: I'll never forget one time, it was in February, I guess, and this old guy come walking up the darn valley. He had a beard, and he was quite an old chap. I thought, "What the heck?" You know, out in that area? What would anybody be doing way out there? He come and knocked on the door. So we let him come in, and it was about three o'clock in the afternoon. And it was cold—oh man, it was cold! So anyway, he come in and he want to know if he could stay overnight. Couldn't get a thing out of [him about] where he was going. He was supposed to be going to Hitchcock. And anyway, he wanted to stay. So okay. But what a miserable old sucker he was. He just about demanded everything. He was an old Scotchman. And he was going to order some goods in town and wanted to make Joyce—if he could get some tweeds from Scotland—he was going to make her a suit.

Joyce Muirhead: Our oldest son saw him

coming. He had a big long white beard. And he said, "Here comes Santa Claus." And he was so excited. His eyes were about this big, you know. And he thought for sure that was Santa Claus.

Jack Muirhead: You know, when I went to town, that old guy, he made sure that I didn't inform anybody that he was there. In fact, I thought of phoning the police, trying to find out about him. Then I thought, "Oh, what the heck. It's none of my business." But anyway, he stayed there and he demanded certain things for his meals and—oh, he was a miserable old fellow. Anyway, he decided that he was going to meet these people in Hitchcock. He was supposed to meet them at a certain time. Okay, so I got the horses and away we went. So anyway—got to the crossroads, and—well, he'd walk now. So I thought, "Okay." So I turned around and he jumped out. He started out towards Hitchcock, and when I got down a ways, I turned around and looked, and he had backtracked and he was going east instead of north. So he stayed at our neighbours that night, I guess. And then he went on, he went east somewhere. I don't know what eventually happened to the old fellow.

✦

Margaret Pick: We had a hired man there when I was six, he was there when I was six years old. And he used to—I can remember—he was a beautiful singer. He come from England and he used to milk the cows, and he always

At one time the Klyne/Blondeau home stood beside the tree in this photograph, and the rocks seen here lined the root cellar. The CPR homestead is visible in the background. *Courtesy Western Heritage Services, Saskatoon*

they slept in the hay-loft, in the hay mow. You'd make your bed on the hay.

✦

Margaret Pick: Mom rode [the herd] with the help of hired men. And they used to come down the railroad track—quite a few of them. Hoboes. And Mom used to always say that they made a sign, because they always seemed to land up at her place. I never found it, but it would work for a while. But they would work, and then they'd go on again, but I don't think they ever got much pay.

sang all the time he was milking. And we used to stand outside the barn and listen to him milk. I used to listen to him sing, and if we went in, he'd stop singing.

✦

Ernie Hanna: We had a couple of guys came up from the States looking for work. They worked for us there at harvest time. IWW, as you called them: "I Won't Work." One was a real good man and the other was an I-Won't-Work man. But the one stayed there and worked for us for quite a while before he left. They just come with a pack on their back. Right on the west side of the house here, we had a couple of bunkhouses just for hired men. But if there wasn't room in the bunkhouse,

Work

The daily work routine on the farm has changed little from the days of the first settlers to more recent times: growing crops, taking care of livestock, and maintaining the farm buildings and equipment. In the early days of settlement, however, self-sufficiency was the rule for almost everyone in the valley.

. . . down on the farm

Jack Muirhead: My granddad used to put up hay by hand. He would be there seven o'clock in the morning, and he'd be standing with his fork, and he had maybe one or two people hired to help him. But he built his stacks by hand. They used to hire a baler to come. They used to sell a lot of feed in some of those years, too.

I think he kept a bunch of horses there one time. They wintered a bunch of horses there for some contractor building roads, you know. And in them days, it was all done with horses. My granddad supplied the feed, and they had hired men there to feed the stock.

✦

Edgar Sawyer: They had everything. Horses and mules. They made their

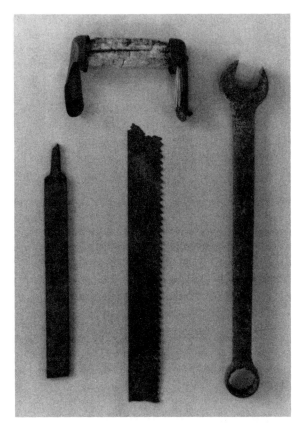

Tools of the trade. Wrench found at the Reddemann farm (SE 1/4 7-3-9 W2). Other artifacts are from the Klyne/Blondeau homestead (SW 1/4 30-3-10 W2). *Courtesy Western Heritage Services, Saskatoon*

living that way, you know. You didn't go to town and get your milk and get your meat and get your butter. You *took* that to town, you know. I've seen my mother come out to the barn with a milk pail to pick the eggs. You'd do that three or four times a day, you know. So that's a lot of eggs.

◆

Helen Blondeau: Well, we had cattle and pigs and chickens—we had all that stuff. Oh yeah, we raised cattle and we raised pigs. So we had all the milk and butter and cream and everything. We had great big churns to churn it—great big churns. And you'd use your feet and your hands to go round and round.

◆

Jack Muirhead: When we first started out, I broke up some of the land, and the first year I grew flax. And I had about twenty bushels to the acre of flax, and it was worth five dollars a bushel in them days. It was really good money. But we started out—we had four cows and we milked and we kept chickens. And we used to buy a pair of pigs, and we'd feed them the milk from the cows. Like the separated milk. And we'd sell eggs and we'd sell cream.

◆

Edgar Sawyer: Well, it would be pretty well the same thing the whole year round, you know. You cleaned your grain at home with an old fanning mill. You stood there and turned that by hand. That would take you a week to do that. Well, then fix up your machinery and your harness—maybe a week or so

of harness-fixing. Oiling it. Oh, there was all these things—it wasn't just for the spring of the year, you know, but it happened all the year around. If it wasn't harness you were fixing, you were fixing something else, you see.

. . . working the land

The river flats in the valley were a mixed blessing for the settlers: the land was good, but there wasn't much of it. Only a small part of any quarter section was river flat; the rest was river, river bank, and stony hillside.

◆

Jack Muirhead: It was very fertile land then in the valley. When there was a poor crop up on the hill, we had the best crop. But when it was a wet year, it was too wet down below. It would grow too lush. I mean the crop wouldn't produce as well as up on top. It seemed like the land was different. It was good land and it raised a lot of what we used to raise. A lot of seed, especially—barley.

◆

Ernie Hanna: The river flat is the best land there is in the country. I mean, you plough all day down there and never hit a stone, unless it's right along next to the hills. But once you get back on top— when they homesteaded—well, so many rocks. I mean, hell, they couldn't plough up enough to make anything.

One of the busiest times of the year, of course, was harvest. This photo, taken in 1942, shows a woman working in the field. A woman's contribution to the family farm often entailed long hours of hard work that extended beyond purely domestic chores. *Courtesy Norman Blondeau, Macoun*

✦

Edgar Sawyer: Oh God. There was so damn many stones, it just seemed like you could pick and pick and pick, and then look back. You know, if you could see that you've accomplished something—but you haven't. There's just as many stones out there. But we used to pick in the spring and in the fall, we used to pick stones with a team and wagon, you know. Well, if you pick five or six loads of stone in a day, well you think you've done something, you see. But then you look at night when you're done and, "Well, where did we pick them stones?" God, it was awful. And some people just bounced over them. Hard on machinery. Wasn't so bad with horses, you know. They would slow down. But on the tractor, you'd get some awful jolts.

...cattle and horses

Raising livestock was a mainstay of the valley farmer. If the valley hills were not good for crops, they served well enough for grazing cattle and horses. The Hanna Ranch had a particularly large horse operation in the early days.

✦

Ernie Boyer: Art Jones lived along the river. And he didn't farm, actually. They used to make their living herding cattle. See there was a lot of prairie—nobody owned that prairie. Government prairie. So they'd lease it for so many years. And then in the summertime, the farmers had no pasture. There was no community pasture. So the Jones family run herd. They may have had three or four hundred head of cattle at one time. And they'd get three to five dollars a head to look after them for the summer. So they were pretty good at riding horseback.

✦

Ernie Hanna: Dad traded a quarter section of land for 180 head of wild horses from out near Aneroid. And Clarence Huff—I think it was Clarence Huff—or

Land that was unsuitable for farming was often used for pasture. Livestock were no more immune to the elements than were people. Here cattle can be seen swimming across a flooded Souris River. *Courtesy Helen Blondeau, Midale*

was it Uncle Ernie?—and Dad, they went out on the train with their saddles. And Dad was supposed to pick out the culls of his herd. But when they got out there late in the fall, well, they just rounded up 180 head or 200—whatever it was—and said, "Take 'em." And they drove them back to Midale, you know.

Breaking wild horses was a specialty of the Hannas, although there were plenty of others in the valley who could also do the job.

✦

Ernie Hanna: That was the roughest ride I ever had. It was out at the rodeo at Aneroid. Uncle Ernie Hanna turned him out—it was his saddle horse, too. He turned him out and let him run for a while. And then he drawed his own saddle horse at the chute and took first

money. And later I rode that horse. We got a hold of him, and I rode him all fall and all winter. And we turned him out and let him run for a month or two— and that was in the thirties where it was so dry, and no feed.

So then we took thirty head or forty head of horses and started north, in order to trade them for hay or whatever. You know, just sell them. We got as far as Lipton, and this kid that worked for us all the time, he said, well if I'd ride him first, he'd ride him the rest of the day. So I rode him in the stockyard, and I couldn't eat for two days! Yeah, if you'd turned him loose, and then you crawled on him again— well, he used to buck every once in a while anyway—but not like that! I mean, he'd go up and you'd think he was going to land on his side. But he'd land one way, and the next time he'd be

The Hannas, seen here on horseback in 1926, started their ranching operation when Ernie Hanna's father, George, traded a quarter section of land for 180 head of wild horses. *Courtesy Clara Ziehl, Midale*

going in the other direction. And he hit the ground so hard that I couldn't eat for two days.

I know one mare—she unloaded me once, because I felt sorry for her. She was fat in the spring and I rode her clear down to Tribune, and she got sore behind the front legs. So I put a rope from the cinch back around behind the saddle to kind of hold it back. And then she kind of got sore up on her shoulders. So when I went to get on her that morning—she was so raw and sore—I hated to cinch the saddle up tight. And I got on, and the first thing you knew, she unloaded me, saddle and all, right over her head, because I didn't have it tight enough. She even took the bridle off. Because

I went over her head. I cinched her up after that. I give up feeling sorry for her.

And God, there was another old bucker that threw me off, and I landed with my feet in the air, and my hands both right smack around a two-by-four. I thought it went clear through me. She bucked backwards underneath the hayrack and tipped the rack off the wagon. Yeah, she unloaded a lot of people.

Sometimes I wonder how I lived that long, you know. But after I got married, the wife, she was so scared all the time. But I broke quite a few after that, though, when she wasn't around.

Looking after cattle meant spending a lot of time in the saddle, not only to round up the livestock, but to make sure that the fence line was in good order.

✦

Margaret Pick: And of course they had to ride the pastures all the time to make sure the fences were up, because there's the cattle and everything all in there.
Gerald Pick: That was darn tough!

Feeding the cattle on the Hanna Ranch was a bit easier in the wintertime, when the cattle would tend to find shelter along the river bank.

✦

Margaret Pick: In wintertime there wasn't a whole lot to it, because right in down here, along the river, we fed the cattle. What cattle we had were fed on the river bank. Not a high bank, but there was a bank all around here. We used to just put the hay down on the ice, and that's how the cattle ate. Actually the cattle didn't go very far.

Winter or summer, however, sick livestock were always a problem. The Hanna Ranch had a special hospital barn.

✦

Ernie Hanna: You know, the cows would be thin and skinny. Some of them, you'd have to help them up. You'd get one of them going and there'd be another one that you'd have to help. Yeah, that's why it was called the "hospital barn," because anything

that was sick, that needed help . . .

A lot of times we'd have horses there, too, that you'd have to lift up, you know, to get up. And I know that Dad's old main saddle horse—I think it was one that he drove up to this country from Iowa—the team and the democrat, when he come up here in 1904— why we found her in the lane down at the straw pile. Every once in a while you'd find one dead in the straw pile, you know. They lay down and roll, and then they couldn't get up. They kind of get on their back. They couldn't get up. And you know, we didn't even recognize her. She'd been laying there so long, she was pawing but she couldn't get rolled up. We rolled her up and got her lifted up. She headed right straight for the buildings. But she was getting pretty old then.

Ranchers in the valley used to send their cattle to the Hanna Ranch for pasturing, and Sunday was the day when they'd come to the ranch to inspect their livestock.

✦

Margaret Pick: All these people that put herd cattle in our pasture. On Sunday, the men would come down to the house and look at their cattle. See how they were doing. It was some place to go. And we'd go out and round them all up. I can remember Dad saying, "That's yours there, John." You know, and then they'd all come in the house and Mom fed them. I don't know how she done it.

Gerald Pick: Sunday afternoon they'd come down and look at the cattle. They did that when I was running it. And it's surprising, when you're in that business, how fellows will come down. They'll send cattle and deny that they own them, after they've been in that pasture for a month. I argued with one guy. I phoned him because his heifer was sick. And when he come down— "Well, that's not mine." I said, "Yes, it is." "No, it ain't." Well, then I started pointing his cattle out and counting them to him, and I said, "She's lost a lot of weight. That's why I wanted you to come down and look at her." "Well, if she's going to live, she's going to live, and if she dies, she dies." He went home. I'll be damned if I didn't lose her.

... pigs and turkeys

Horses and cattle weren't the only livestock. Almost everyone in the valley raised a few pigs. Generally, farmers kept a sow for breeding and sold off the young pigs once they were fattened up.

✦

Ernie Hanna: Well, those pigs pretty much raised theirselves. I mean they got away up there to Monsons—that's a mile and a half or better—where they got into their garden patch. But they had the river banks all rooted up, and whatever roots they were getting, golly, I mean, they grew up! Well just the last while, you put them in the corral and feed them, before you sold them. But we would just go down with a saddle horse and round them up and chase them back. Yeah, round them up and put them in the corral there in the fall.

✦

Jack Muirhead: Oh, there's another story about the darned pigs. I'll never forget that! We went out to this guy to get a pair of pigs. And I don't know why I thought of a pair. I guess maybe I wanted a pair, but I didn't have enough money. I think I had ten dollars. It cost me ten dollars. So I took one pig. And we come home with it, and the blamed thing got away on us. I don't know—I guess the kids, the neighbour kids and our oldest boy, left the door of the shed open, and the pig got away on us. That was the end of the pig. We never did find it.

Turkey farming was another way of making some money.

✦

Ernie Boyer: And then Art Jones used to raise a lot of turkeys. They called him "Turkey Jones." He'd raise maybe a couple of hundred turkeys. He was a big nuisance to us because his turkeys would come into our field and clean up the wheat. The darn things would fly across the river. They got so they could fly, and you see, our field was across the river. But after a while he cut the wings on them so they wouldn't be able to fly.

. . . construction work

Not all the work in the valley was on the ranch or farm. In order to make some much-needed extra money, the men often hired themselves out for local roadwork and other construction jobs.

✦

Jack Boyer: We'd go out and work on the road to pay our taxes, which we done for years. Get four horses and a fresno [a kind of dirt-scooper], or put them on a grader or something. South of us was

bad. You know, try to build a road in there and, boy, that was tough digging. But north of the river, it was pretty good. You know, it was easy to work on the road there. That road south—oh boy! It was terrible.

✦

Gerald Pick: Tommy Douglas, when he was in power, they built that dam straight south of Midale. And he said that down there would be a place to put a dam, but there wasn't equipment or nothing else to bank that river like there is now. That dam was put in with horses, that one down there by Midale.

Margaret Pick: They killed a lot of good horses on that dam. They had these—what did they call them?—shovel things they had on behind the horses that scraped the dirt.

Gerald Pick: Like a grader, but only pulled by horses. It was kind of like your front-end bucket on your tractor with a handle on it. You had four horses ahead of it and you scooped it forward and pushed down on the handle.

✦

The Midale Dam, pictured here in 1944, still stands today. Horses were used in the construction of the dam, and according to some people a good number of the animals died in the process. *Courtesy Norman Blondeau, Macoun*

. . . resourcefulness

Very little went to waste on the farm. If something could be reused or refashioned, it was. Resourcefulness was the key to keeping the family farm running properly.

✦

Ernie Hanna: Five or six of us sitting around after supper in the house. And each bring in a chunk of railroad tie and lay it down, you know, and then straightening nails. Pull the nails out and save them all, and straighten the nails to reuse the nails again, you know.

✦

Jack Muirhead: One time, we sent a can of cream in, and a mouse had got into it, you know, and we went to pick up our cheque. Well, instead, we get our can of cream back. So Joyce wasn't satisfied with that. She churned it and got the butter and made soap. Soap! Of course they'd pour that dye, that yellow dye, into the cream. I had a lot of yellow shirts, I'll tell you.

Joyce Muirhead: You were lucky you had a shirt.

Jack Muirhead: But I tell you—she wasn't throwing the cream away. No damn way!

Joyce Muirhead: Well, we couldn't afford to throw it away. You see, I depended on that cheque from the cream to buy soap and buy things for the house. The money wasn't there. I had no soap. I had to wash the clothes. So what do you do? You use your head, you make some soap. I had a year's supply of soap!

And it was lye soap, I made, you know. But this dye got into some of the white material—absorbed the dye. But anyway, I used it because we had to. We didn't have the money to run and buy a box of soap every time a mouse got in the cream. And I laugh about that now. I was devastated, then. I didn't know what I was going to do with this can of cream. I couldn't think of wasting anything. And I knew how you make soap—I saw my mother make it.

✦

Ernie Boyer: No, we didn't buy much tinned stuff—probably jam and syrup was most of the cans with lids on. Oh, we used to use a lot of them syrup cans.

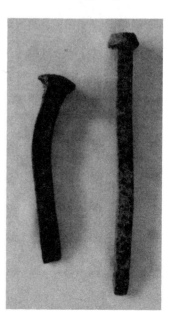

Even railway spikes were recycled, though no one would have called it that back then. They would be gathered up, straightened, then reused. These spikes were found on the Hanna Ranch and Hinzman homestead (SW 1/4 7-3-9 W2). *Courtesy Western Heritage Services, Saskatoon*

I used to use one to go to school with, for my lunch! Carried my lunch in a syrup can—a pretty good-sized one with a handle on it. Easy to carry. And used it for hauling water, too.

"Lunch buckets." *Courtesy Midale Museum*

The women worked at least as hard as the men did, and their labour was just as important to the running of the farm.

✦

Hazel Molstad: Do you want to know what I did? Milked cows, fed chickens, fed pigs, raked hay, stacked—stood in the stack and stacked it. Is that enough? I also stooked.

✦

Edgar Sawyer: They worked. They milked cows and washed clothes and they worked. Raised a family, you know. They didn't run to the store and buy things, and eat out of cans. They canned their own stuff. Well, there's a lot of work to making a meal, you know, for a family. The way they make it today, well if you got a can-opener you're well away, you see.

What is so interesting about an old tin can? You can find them anywhere, right? . . . Wrong. The archaeological survey turned up almost no tin can fragments. This would suggest that the people of this area were very self-sufficient and raised rather than bought their food. What they did buy was usually purchased in bulk. Marion homestead (NW 1/4 10-3-10 W2). *Courtesy Western Heritage Services, Saskatoon*

✦

Carl Hauglum: Wash clothes, churn butter.
Margaret Hauglum: Well, scrubbing on the board—wash clothes with a board and a stomper, you know.
Carl Hauglum: Before they had washing machines. We did it too, first started out.

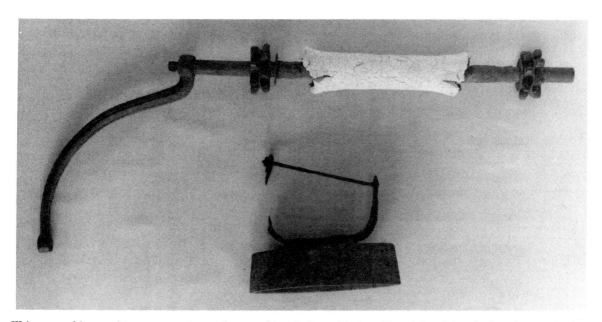

Wringer washing machines were a step up from washing clothes with a washboard, but doing the laundry remained a formidable task for the women. This piece from a wringer washing machine (top) and the iron were found on the Lajimodiere homestead (NE 1/4 16-3-10 W2). *Courtesy Western Heritage Services, Saskatoon*

Margaret Hauglum: Yeah, I washed clothes with boards until Karen was two years old. And I don't know. Of course you'd always have to have a big garden, I guess. And set the eggs under the chickens so you'd have small chicks. And turkeys.

✦

Margaret Pick: Mom used to wash the wool and hang it on the barbed-wire fence to dry. Wash it and wash it and wash it. And then our job was to take it and pick it apart, and get all those little sticks and stuff. And then she'd card it. I still have the carders yet. Carded and carded. She'd card it into bats.

Gerald Pick: Sew it into quilts.

Margaret Pick: And put it into quilts.

✦

Marceline Lajimodiere: I used to milk seven cows. When my kids were small— Harold was twenty-two months old when Vera was born. From June to October, I used to bring the baby carriage in the barn. And Harold used to stand there and watch, so the chickens don't come to the baby, whilst I was milking seven cows. Then I had to haul. Seven cows with eight pails of milk—one of the cows gave two pails of milk. Big, big pails. And I had to haul all that to the house and pass that milk in the cream separator. By hand. Then haul that skim milk again back for the pigs and for the calves.

Although herding and tending the crops might be thought of as "man's work," the women also had to help with these chores on the family farm.

✦

Esther Hanna: Yeah, I remember I used to have to herd the cattle down there when my husband was gone. Then I'd get on horseback. It was a big adventure.

✦

Margaret Pick: My mother used to ride horseback with a big riding skirt. She never wore pants—this great big skirt. Yeah, that's what she used to wear. If she didn't have help, she done a lot of things. Riding.
Wayne Pick: She did a lot of checking cattle and everything.
Margaret Pick: Oh yes. You wonder how she could do it, you know.
Gerald Pick: Yes. The first time I seen Mrs. Hanna, she still cut by hand.

✦

Bella Gardipie: Mom used to tend to the garden. She'd help when haying time came. She used to cut the hay with the mower and Dad used to stack it. My sister, older sister, used to rake it when she was big enough. I was the cook.

✦

John Dowhanuik: When we started to farm a little bit, we had a binder and you'd cut grain. Mom would go out there and stook the grain. Go out and make hay. She helped Dad make hay. The women in the valley were homesteaders, you know! She was always in there pitching hay.

Widows had an especially hard time in the valley. The Muirheads recall one neighbour who worked herself to exhaustion retrieving wood after a flood.

✦

Joyce Muirhead: She brought up three little kids all by herself. She built their barn out of the old trestle. Yeah. And she ruined her back. She ended up in a wheelchair and couldn't move. Just from all that work. And she did that alone. Dragged those great big timbers and everything for the basement of the barn. You know, the courage that woman had was tremendous.
Jack Muirhead: The flood came down, and it was washing away some of the material. She spent all day in that cold water, pulling the timber out to the shore. I think that's what hurt her back.

. . . children's chores

The children also had their chores. They were expected to help around the farm as soon as they were able.

✦

Ernie Boyer: We done what my dad would do. Everything. When I was ten years old, eight, nine, from eight to ten years old I used to milk probably three or four cows, skimmed milk, and feed the calves. Everybody had their job. When I got to be ten years old, I got to working in the field. Drive three horses on the plough, one single-furrow plough. Three horses on it. I used to drive that.

✦

Edgar Sawyer: Well, kids picked eggs and they pumped water and they milked cows, if they were able to carry a pail. And cleaned barns—all these things. They were done every day, this stuff.

✦

Helen Blondeau: Well, we used to learn to knit, and we knitted stockings and mitts and all those things. When we were young, I remember my mother used to teach us to knit. Well, after we got older—us kids—we had to go and milk cows. And feed pigs and calves and chickens. I think we learned to milk when we were about seven years old. We always had about ten or twelve cows to milk. We didn't have no milking machines—*we* were the milking machines.

✦

Bella Gardipie: I was the second oldest, so I had plenty to do. We didn't have time to be bored. I had to look after the smaller children. There was twelve of us in the family. And we had to help with the chores. We had to milk cows and get the cows in. Tended chickens. Whatever there was to do.

Prairie children were very accustomed to hearing the sound of cowbells. By the time they were seven most of them knew how to milk a cow, and chores were a part of everyday life for children and adults alike. This cowbell was found on the Hinzman farm (SW 1/4 7-3-9 W2). *Courtesy Western Heritage Services, Saskatoon*

✦

Edgar Sawyer: Well, I can remember milking cows when I was about seven, maybe younger than that. I could milk, but I couldn't carry the pail. Once it got full, then my mother would come and take that pail and give me another one, you see.

✦

Duane Boyer: Dad believed the best cure for rambunctiousness was hard work. We always had our evening chores to do. I remember one instance of milking a cow after dark when it was very cold.

I was about nine years old at the time. Dad would put us to work building corrals, constructing granaries, and fixing anything in need. These things helped my decision not to farm. Or maybe it was shovelling barley in a granary in midsummer while the grain auger filled the building. (excerpt from *Memories*)

◆

Gerald Pick: Well, down there where the livestock watered out of the river, it was our job to pump the horse trough full of water. Carry wood.
Margaret Pick: Yeah, we carried wood, too, I guess.

◆

Hazel Molstad: Well, the kids helped with the chores.
Arnold Molstad: Milked cows.
Hazel Molstad: And then there's always the little job of getting the kindling wood to start the fire.
Arnold Molstad: That was a big job.
Hazel Molstad: They'd yell, "It's not *my* turn."

◆

Clara Ziehl: And we used to go and have a round-up, and take care of the milk cows. We used to ride miles and miles— you never knew where they were, you know. Great big pasture north or south of the river. You ride and ride and ride and look for them cows. Sometimes we'd find them, sometimes we wouldn't.

◆

Margaret Pick: Sometimes the cattle would be across the river over here in the pasture, and we'd go get them to milk. And we didn't want to go down here. We used to put our feet up on top of the saddle and swim our horses across. And we still couldn't swim. And not one of us ever was in any danger in the water. You know, none of us near drowned or anything, I don't think. And still I'm scared of water.

◆

Clara Ziehl: I used to have to go and help round up cattle, too. My brother and I, we used to go quite often. I remember one time I went, and I didn't want to stay at this one place, because they had lots of dogs. And I said to Dad, "We're not going to stay overnight with these people?" "No, we won't stay there to-night." But sure enough, when we got there, it was just about time to go to bed. So we had to sleep there. I'm telling you.

◆

Margaret Pick: We used to race. Oh yes. We used to go out and round up the cattle with Dad when guys would come down there Sunday to look at their cattle. And they always had these big Hereford bulls running around. And I often think of them, because what chance did we have on horseback? And those bulls would paw the ground, and dust would fly, and they'd bellow.

You'd just keep hollering and yelling. But they didn't do nothing.

◆

Margaret Pick: Oh, I don't know. It seems to me my dad always found one horse for me that wouldn't do nothing for the rest of them, and put me on. He had a little black one. She'd go as far as that gate and she'd stop. And of course I'd get so mad, and you'd try pulling her, and she'd just turn her head around and go back. And then my brother would get on with spurs, and she'd go for him. I'd get back on. And then if they get her a little ways away from the house, she'd go to school. And by that time the rest of them had all gone ahead.

◆

Rose Boyer Overold: When I was fourteen I first started working out for Mr. and Mrs. Reddemann. Believe me, I had to work. I had to milk thirteen cows, bake bread, and do almost everything else that came along. In the fall, Walter Reddemann gave Pa a wagonload of potatoes for my wages. (excerpt from *Memories*)

. . . threshing

Perhaps the hardest work of the year was threshing. Getting the crop in and taking the grain to town involved all the family members, as well as any hired help that the family could afford.

◆

Carl Hauglum: Yeah, threshing meant a big day. Daylight till sunset, by the time you get your chores done. Had to haul a lot of bundles. Big outfits—had twelve teams on that outfit that we had, and a spike pitcher and a field pitcher besides to help you to load up, and you get another to help you unload. The spike pitcher is the man that helped you unload bundles. And there was a guy below the feeder, too, to keep the feeder from spilling over—keep the spill from piling up. There was one guy to fire the steam engines. Another to haul the straw back, to keep poking straw to keep the steam up. They call him the straw monkey. Yeah, that's what they called him. And the water hauler. That was a big crew—twenty-four men.

◆

Edgar Sawyer: We started work at four o'clock in the morning, lots and lots and lots of mornings. Harvest time was the worst, you know. Then when you got a threshing outfit—we had an outfit of our own—why you never slept. Only just a little now and then. The farmers would haul bundles, you see, but we'd do their threshing. My brother-in-law, he had a steam outfit. You had to have a fireman. You had to have a water flunky, you know, to haul water. Then you had to have a straw flunky—one to haul the straw to keep the steam up. Yes, those outfits were a lot of work. And then you had to get up

39

at half-past three, four o'clock in the morning to get enough steam so you could move the rig, you know.

✦

Ernie Hanna: We'd haul all the stuff up and stack it there. And threshed enough oats for feed and stuff, and some wheat, probably, or barley. And then we'd have the straw pile right there. I mean you'd haul it across the field and stack it near the corrals. And then they'd try to move the threshing machines in. They'd move the threshing outfit from place to place, too.

✦

This threshing machine, owned by the Boyers, was one of few in the area in the early years, and was hired out to other farmers during threshing time. These folks also found it to be a good spot for a photograph (1942). *Courtesy Norman Blondeau, Macoun*

Helen Blondeau: Yeah. Dad always used to have a threshing machine. He'd always thresh. Ever since I could remember. He used to have a steam engine at one time—when I first remember. And he used that for years and years. And then he got a different threshing machine—gasoline powered. He'd go all over and thresh. And they'd have a cook car when they'd go threshing.

He'd have a crew—he'd have eight or nine men and they go on in the cook car. And away they'd go. They'd hire somebody to cook, or my sister used to cook when she got old enough—my oldest sister. And her cousin. Yeah, they'd go cooking for the threshers. And they'd go threshing all over. One time it snowed and they had to quit threshing for about two weeks. There was a lot of snow. Well, I suppose they'd thresh later in the year than they combine now. The hired hands—some of these guys would come along looking for jobs. And Dad would hire a couple of them. And then from the valley there'd be Molstads coming there, and Laroques—the Laroques would come. Steinke—Leonard Steinke lived not far from our place.

◆

Jack Boyer: Well, the worst job was pitching and bundling, I guess. It was hard work, anyway. You know you rubbed your hands raw. Wouldn't think of doing it today.

◆

Carl Hauglum: Which was the worst job? I don't know. Grain-haulers had the hardest job. They had to shovel. No augers them days. They had to throw the grain higher than their heads. They had to throw up so it wouldn't fall.

◆

Edgar Sawyer: Oh yeah. Mom had to feed the whole crew, you know. They'd sleep in the barn or sleep in the granary or any place.

◆

Arnold Molstad: Threshing was hard on the women.
Hazel Molstad: At threshing you had to cook. I remember once, we cooked for twelve men for three days. Three meals a day plus two lunches every day. You're really busy!

◆

Ernie Boyer: Women would make big roasts for the thresh crew. Seem like to me it was a pretty good meal. And they used to make pies by the dozen. There was twenty men there looking for a piece of pie. Yeah, they had to cook for them from morning till night. Make bread. Oh, it was quite an operation.

Durable prairie china—an enamel cup found on the Reddemann farm (SE 1/4 7-3-9 W2). *Courtesy Western Heritage Services, Saskatoon*

◆

Marceline Lajimodiere: I only weighed

122 pounds when my kids were small, and I had twenty-two men to cook for. And my baby, Vera, was creeping. And no electricity then. Just wood and coal and everything. Give them breakfast, and ten o'clock lunch. I had to fix a big basketful of sandwiches, and tea or coffee—whatever they want to drink. Big pots full. I had to take that over to the field. If I couldn't go, then somebody from the threshing outfit came and got the lunch. That was at ten o'clock. Then I had to have the dinner—usually be at twelve o'clock. Supper was—well I told them: "You have to have supper at six o'clock, because I have too much work to do after supper." The cows got to be milked now, again. Of course Albert was home then, when they were threshing at home. He used to milk the cows. But I had to look after the milk and the cream. And so they used to come at six o'clock and eat. And I had the whole evening to myself. And the people that was hauling grain, they used to bring the meat, fresh meat from Macoun. Seven miles. Because where we were, you couldn't keep the meat, fresh meat, any place. Sometimes I used to cook chickens and stuff. Had to make pies. Vera was creeping.

Oh, we always had a garden. We had to. One time the threshers were at home, so I pulled a little wagon—Vera was born in June and this was in the fall—threshing time. I put her in the wagon and pulled her in the garden. And my son, Harold, was walking. I went and got a pumpkin to make a

pumpkin pie. I would say about thirty years after, I was in the hardware store here in Estevan, and one of the clerks—he had grey hair—said, "This is the woman that can make pumpkin pie." And I said, "How do you know?" And he said, "Do you remember the time you lived in the big white house?"—that's where Vera was born. He said, "I was loading—" They were threshing. They used to load the bundles by hand, you know, with a team of horses and a hay rack. "I was moving with my load there and I saw you going with a little wagon with your little baby in it, and the little boy was walking behind. And then you came with the pumpkin. The best pumpkin pie I ever had. There was this much whipped cream on it. I could have ate the whole pie!" I didn't remember him, but he said he was only about eighteen years old at the time. Now he was an old man, you see.

. . . gardening

But harvesting extended beyond the work of threshing. Just about everyone in the valley had a garden, and a good harvest of vegetables and fruit in the fall meant that there would be plenty of food for the family through the winter months. Most people in the valley will tell you that the responsibility for the garden fell on the women—from planting in the spring to canning the produce in late fall.

◆

Helen Blondeau: Oh yeah, we had lots of

The cans lined up on the windowsill here contain seedlings. Started early in the spring, the young plants would be transplanted to the garden once the risk of frost was over. On the prairies, deciding when that point has arrived is anyone's guess. *Courtesy Norman Blondeau, Macoun*

pounds. It was a big garden.

✦

Helen Blondeau: Yeah, that was sure good ground to make gardens, down there. The gardens would just *grow*. It seemed like a lot better than around here. Around here I think it's too sandy or something. There it was kind of gumbo, and when you stepped on it then your shoes got as big as a house. Yeah, we'd always have the garden right beside the river. But after the dykes—they built dykes there in the dirty thirties—well, then the gardens weren't there no more. So I can't remember—oh, we had a garden across the river—a little spot there. That was good, too.

✦

big gardens. We put our garden along the river. Oh, our potatoes and everything. I don't think we used to water them. I guess it would just rain lots.

✦

Ernie Hanna: And then the garden was the ground where you used to plant corn and sunflowers and potatoes and stuff—from there clear down to the river.

✦

Ernie Boyer: We'd raise, maybe, a couple of hundred bushels of potatoes, turnips—carrots by the thousand

✦

Uncle Ernie Hanna: Oh, everything Mom would use in the house. They raised a lot. All of their vegetables alone. Garden cabbage and carrots and peas and beans and everything like that. And they canned it down, a lot of them.

◆

Margaret Pick: You got peas and carrots. Mom had always canned our own vegetables.

Gerald Pick: There wasn't this broccoli and cauliflower that you had to start in the house and grow. There was peas and beans and carrots and turnips.

◆

Joyce Muirhead: We usually had a fair garden. I used to can five hundred sealers every year of corn and peas and beans—everything—beets, whatever was there, I canned it. Because we had no deep freeze or anything, you know.

Jack Muirhead: Raspberries and strawberries—not strawberries. We didn't have strawberries. But raspberries.

Joyce Muirhead: We had raspberries, I remember that.

Jack Muirhead: Saskatoons.

◆

Helen Blondeau: And Grandma had a garden there. Oh, she used to have a lot of raspberries and a lot of those little bushes, like raspberries and black currants, and all that in her garden. I remember that. That was great.

◆

Ernie Hanna: My uncle would come down with little trees. I kind of half-remember—I don't know whether I'd be two or three years old—whatever—and he planted them two trees. One on each side of the well there. But by the time we left, they were getting pretty thick. Now they're dead and somebody's cut them off.

. . . hunting and trapping

Hunting and trapping were a part of the work year for some people in the valley. Deer were scarce (especially before the late thirties), but wild birds and rabbits were plentiful. Of course, wild game was a supplement to the family's diet, but most hunting and trapping was done for the furs. Farmers trapped muskrat, beaver, weasels, and even mink along the river. After skinning the carcasses, they would clean and stretch the hides, and then sell the pelts to the fur merchants.

◆

Wayne Pick: You couldn't get a much better trapper or hunter than Uncle Henry. He had hounds.

Margaret Pick: He had hounds.

Wayne Pick: Some lead dogs and a killer.

Margaret Pick: One time I was upstairs and I came down and I said, "There's a coyote over there." "Let's go," Henry said. So we jumped in the old car and away we went. And the hounds were in the back seat—three of them. And the window was open, and he was going to say, "Don't let the dogs out," when out the window they went. They spotted this coyote. And it sure wasn't very long till they had him. And one hound that grabbed his throat, you know. And when we got there, Henry called them off. Then he got the dogs back in the back seat again, and they were panting right over my head—and all covered with blood.

✦

Ernie Boyer: Then in the forties the deer come in—or in the late thirties. About '35. Started to come in. Well, by the mid-forties, there was a lot of deer. You could go out and shoot one any time.

✦

Edgar Sawyer: Yup. It was in the wintertime. A deer come running through the yard. We were eating breakfast. Gee, everybody got up and outside there to see that thing. And then it went down to the neighbour's. So on the phone: "Here comes a deer." Well hell, in them days, you know there weren't many deer in the area. I guess they come from the mountains or wherever—straggled in. But now it's often you see a deer.

✦

Gerald Pick: All the boys were trapping. While they were home, they were trapping for their folks.
Margaret Pick: They all helped.
Gerald Pick: They all sold the hides, and their mother got the money to buy groceries. That was just the common thing.

Deer were scarce in the Souris Valley area until the mid-1930s, but there were plenty of wild birds and rabbits to be had. *Courtesy Souris Basin Development Authority*

Gerald and Margaret Pick: Muskrats and beaver.
Gerald Pick: Any kind of coyotes.

✦

Helen Blondeau: My husband used to trap minks down the river. Oh yeah, those minks and beavers. And muskrats in the spring. Yeah, my brothers used to kill muskrats, too. They were easy to kill, muskrats. They'd go and set a trap there. But you have to watch them, because they'd break their leg easy. They just had a little thin leg. I don't know if they chewed them off or what, but my brothers'd have to set them and then go see them at night before they went to bed, and then again

This part of an old gun was found on the Lajimodiere homestead (NE 1/4 16-3-10 W2), and the cartridge on the Reddemann farm (SE 1/4 7-3-9 W2). Very few gun remains were discovered, probably because most guns were well maintained by their owners. *Courtesy Western Heritage Services, Saskatoon*

in the morning, real early, or their muskrats would be gone. Yeah, their legs would be either chewed off or something.

My brothers used to snare rabbits. Yeah, there was an awful lot of rabbits one year. They used to have rabbit drives, eh? A bunch of people would go together. Oh, there was just hundreds of rabbits. I don't know where they disappeared to. When they'd snare them, they'd snare them in the bushes. But I don't know how they'd leave their snares, because there they'd come out with rabbits anyway. And we'd go along with them, and there they'd come out with a nice white rabbit. I guess they were easy to snare. Fifty cents a rabbit without skinning them. They'd just sell them like that.

✦

Wayne Pick: Uncle Henry trapped. I can

remember going there in the wintertime, and he'd be downstairs, you know, skinning and pulling pelts.

Margaret Pick: You just put the trap— fastened it on to a board and run it out into the river and tie it.

Wayne Pick: Yeah, leg-hold traps.

Margaret Pick: And then you tie the board to the trees along the edge. And when Kurt—we had our older son— when he'd go to sleep, I'd go out on the trap lines. And they'd be caught in the trap and then they'd jump off and drown, eh? And then we'd skin them, and then of course the buyer come to Estevan. The inspector would come along, and the buyer'd get him drunk, and then turn around and buy hides when he was sleeping it off.

Gerald Pick: But we were trapping to live.

Margaret Pick: To live, you bet we were doing it! I don't know what we got—a dollar and a quarter or some stupid thing for a hide.

Gerald Pick: That buyer was good. He bought from Henry and he bought from everybody when it was against the law to do it. But he always gave us a pretty good price for hides. He didn't say, "You guys are stuck. I'll give you ten cents"—not him. He payed for them. Then he hauled them into Manitoba, where it was legal to catch them. That's where he got rid of them.

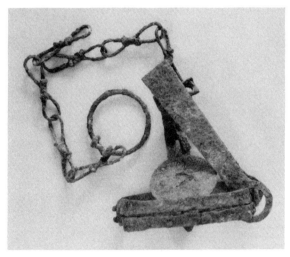

Muskrats, beavers, weasels, coyotes, mink, and even gophers were among the animals trapped for their hides (and tails). Almost every family did some trapping. This old leg-hold trap was discovered on the Hinzman farm (SW 1/4 7-3-9 W2). *Courtesy Western Heritage Services, Saskatoon*

✦

Carl Hauglum: One winter on the farm we lived on—farmed east of here about two and a half miles. We had to go some place. I had to come home that evening. I got up in the morning, here's

this nice shiny animal in the trap. I didn't know what the dickens it was until I picked it up: "It's a mink!" Because minks were rare. And I skinned it and stretched it and took it to Estevan, and they only wanted to give me a couple of bucks for it. "No," I said, "I'll never sell it. I'll keep it for a souvenir." Mink were rare in the country, you know. And I kept it for a few weeks. Then I sent it to a government fur company. I got forty bucks for it. The bastard in Estevan would only give me two bucks. He thought I was green. I was a kid, too, you know—maybe twenty-five or something like that.

✦

Margaret Pick: But at that time, Uncle Henry was hard up. So he trapped. Of course that was his life. And he had all these rats on stretchers in the house, and my other sister lived way over by Goodwater, and she had to go through long distance from Goodwater to Midale and to him. And they didn't have a phone—Henry there. But Mrs. Affie did down at Elswick. And they told her to go and tell Uncle Henry that the police were coming. Well, she had pretty near half a mile to go. And when she got there, she said, "The police are coming!" So he headed upstairs and grabbed all these pelts and put them in bed, and she got in bed with them—the old girl. Mrs. Affie. And the police didn't look very good then. So then they went on in their car and they went south for just a little while, and they come back. By that time Henry had thrown a bunch of the pelts in front of a colt that was wild anyway, and of course she was worse with the smell of these rats.

Gerald Pick: All of them fresh hides.

Margaret Pick: So he grabbed them all, and I guess he threw a bunch of stretchers in the stove and everything else with it. And by the time the police came back, he had got them all out and had hidden them in the slough. But the police had went to the barn, the first time, and they had went through the house a certain amount when they came back. And they said, "You are warned!" They made Henry take everything out in front of those horses. They wouldn't go in the barn.

Gerald Pick: By that time it was safe to do it.

Margaret Pick: But gee I would have loved to have a movie of that. That would have been something to see.

Gerald Pick: You made damn sure they didn't see the traps. You see, a muskrat is the stupidest thing in the world to trap. And they would go out swimming in the evening. So you're pretty sure there's going to be no inspector. So you take your traps, and in the morning, you take them on in and hide them. But you can get ten, fifteen rats in a couple of hours, because they're curious. And that board floating on the water—they got to jump on there.

Hides and the stretchers. You hang them someplace where they're out of sight. They'd dry quicker in the house than in the barn. You put up with the smell when you need the money.

Margaret Pick: It didn't take long to dry.

Gerald Pick: You see it's in the spring of the year when that hide don't dry outside.

◆

Jack Muirhead: Our neighbour was quite a trapper. He used to trap muskrats.

Joyce Muirhead: Well, that finished me!

Jack Muirhead: So we thought we'd trap. And I never trapped in my life.

Joyce Muirhead: I never did, too.

Jack Muirhead: Anyway, we thought we'd buy a dozen traps and trap some of these. And I'm still not a trapper— I'll tell you that. I think maybe we caught enough muskrats to pay for the doggone traps, and that's about all. I couldn't prepare the fur.

Joyce Muirhead: Well you see, I was born and brought up in the Qu'Appelle Valley. And my brothers—that's all the money we had was from furs. I had a .22 when I was just a little girl. And we used to go out and shoot the muskrats—not trap them. I don't like trapping them. That's cruel. If you're going to kill them, kill them.

Do you remember the time I fell off the muskrat house? My son Owen thought I was drowning.

◆

Carl Hauglum: I trapped weasels and rabbits and stuff like that. In the wintertime.

Margaret Hauglum: He trapped gophers for the tails.

Carl Hauglum: Oh, I trapped a lot of gophers, too. Got a cent or two per tail or something like that. Lot of gophers in them days. Some would get up to a hundred gophers, and then bring them in. And some of them had a trick to cut the tails in half. So they'd have two of them for one. We did it with rats here, too. Double up their tails. The councillor didn't care. You'd bring in your bag. He took your word for it—he didn't want to dig in and count all those dirty tails. He paid you for the bag depending on what you said it was. Kept the kids going, you know.

. . . fishing

It's debatable whether fishing in the river, creeks, and lakes of the valley was work or pleasure, but it was certainly another source of food. Fishing, from shore in warm weather or in a hut on the ice in the winter, was one activity that everyone in the valley could take part in.

✦

Carl Hauglum: Like Dad's homestead was close to the lake. If you didn't have much food in hand, you go down to the lake and swing a line in and bring home fish. That was for supper or dinner. That would be jackfish—most of them—in them days. There might be the odd pickerel down there, too. Yeah. There were a lot of fish and a lot of water in them days, too.

✦

Gerald Pick: Yeah, there is catfish in some of the lakes. Canadians throw them away and Americans eat them.

✦

Jack Boyer: Yeah, I remember years ago, it was a wonderful way to live. You could fish pretty near any place in the river, and there was always muskrats and beaver and ducks and geese. Well, there was even goldeyes down there. Yeah, pickerel and jackfish and the suckers—perch. Goldeyes. I remember catching goldeyes. And after the water dried up, all that stuff disappeared. Even the ducks have gone.

✦

Edgar Sawyer: Oh, jacks and suckers—that's mostly all. But that place was just loaded—on Sundays it was just lousy with people come down to fish. Cut an old willow and tie a string on it and a hook, and throw it in.

✦

Norman Blondeau: But I do remember—there were quite a number of trees between the house and towards the bank of the river. That's where we used to get our fishing poles from. The trees were so nice.

✦

Edgar Sawyer: Oh yeah. Fishhouse on the ice. Yes, a lot of good fishing there. Oh, you just build a little thing, like an outhouse, you know. And throw it on the sleigh and take it down and shove it on the ice. Just to get out of the wind.

◆

Helen Blondeau: Yeah, we liked to go fishing. Down at Mainprize Park we used to fish lots, but then the river went quite dry. Well, there hasn't been any fish for the last couple of years. And we'd go and catch fish on the ice down on the river. Yeah, we had little ice houses, little ice houses all over the place. In the spring they'd have to pull them off the ice or they'd sink in. They'd have to pull them off—take them home, I guess. They weren't that big. They could put them on their truck and take them home. Some of them were quite big, but some were just small ones that they could just sit in and make an ice hole and sit there. Make a little fire.

◆

Arnold Molstad: Oh yeah, there was quite a few ice houses, but there was a lot of open fishing, too. I mean, just chop a hole and fish. This here old fellow, Faggetter. They took him and threw him in jail one time for fishing without a licence. But Archie Barbour went in and took him back out.

In the early days, when the water level of the Souris River was higher, fish were plentiful and an important, if sometimes monotonous, addition to the dinner table. People often built ice houses to fish from during the winter months, though none can be seen in this 1954 photo. *Courtesy Helen Blondeau, Midale*

Water and Fire in the Valley

The two elements that define the valley are water and coal. The Souris River and its small tributaries, as well as the lakes, dykes, and dams that form the valley's water system make the area a very different place from the flat prairielands beyond. As well, the coal seams, large and small, which run through the hills of the valley, have not only shaped its industrial history, but have played a part in the daily lives of many who made the valley their home.

. . . drinking water

Providing drinking water for both people and animals was always a concern of the valley people. While there was usually plenty of water in the river suitable for livestock, drinking water had to come from wells and springs.

✦

Marceline Lajimodiere: We had to haul drinking water. All our water was alkali. It was okay for the animals, you know, but it was no good for the house. So we had to go about a mile from our well towards the river, where somebody had a well there. People had wells. And we used to haul water in cream cans. And for washing, you used to haul it from the river—that was soft water to do the washing. But for cooking, we got water from a neighbour's well.

✦

Ernie Hanna: Our well was about twenty-five feet deep, and it was about six feet square, to start with. When it started caving, why we went in and made a new curbing. Put down in there about four foot square. We used to have to go down and clean it every once in a while. Somebody'd make a mistake and tip the milk or cream over into the well. You'd have to pump the water out and go down and clean the well out again. It got so that sometimes it was pretty dangerous to go down and clean it out. So we put a new curbing inside again, because if it caved in while you were down there, there'd be no way of ever digging you out by hand. Well, the water used to get up there quite deep, too. I don't know; I imagine the water used to probably come up six or eight feet deep in it.

✦

Ernie Boyer: Yeah, some had pumps,

some just hauled the water up with rope and a pulley. We had too much water, so we had to have a pump, and you'd get quite a bit for stock. And we drank that water, too. Oh well, you'd get bugs, and frogs, and snakes, and whatnot with it. You'd just drain them out, screen them out, and there was your drinking water. To clean the well, we'd take all the water out, and take all these snakes and bugs out. But a lot of the wells had good covers on them, so that not too much would get in. We had a fairly decent well, a fairly good well, and we had a cement top on it, and it was pretty well sealed. We didn't have too much problem. We used it a lot for cattle and other animals. The well pulled water out from the side hill—it would run in from the side hill—and it would go right through down below. It would never stop! So our water was pure and fresh all the time.

◆

Margaret Pick: But washing clothes on the washboard—that was quite a job. We used river water down there. We hauled it up with pails. I don't think I ever remember using well water for dishes or anything.

◆

Joyce Muirhead: We had no water in the house until '63. We used to carry it—bring it from the river in a barrel or pump it and bring it, and heat it on the coal stove. No electricity.

Jack Muirhead: We had a well. We built a well.

Joyce Muirhead: We had a well but it was hard water—spring water—and that's no good to wash diapers. So we had to go down to the river.

Pails were a multi-purpose item on the farm. Drinking water often had to be hauled from a neighbour's if a family did not have their own well or spring. This bucket was found on the Hinzman farm (SW 1/4 7-3-9 W2). *Courtesy Western Heritage Services, Saskatoon*

◆

Gerald Pick: There was a lot of wells for the stock water, but not for drinking.

Margaret Pick: But if we go to do dishes or anything, we'd just go get a pail of water from the river. If there were bugs and stuff on it, you'd skim them off with the pail and then dip.

Gerald Pick: Pretty near everybody had a cistern in their house, under their house, and a few good wells that had real good water.

Margaret Pick: Then they'd have a pump to pump the water up from the cistern. I got one there sitting on the window.

Gerald Pick: The cisterns were made out of brick, and then in there was charcoal, and your pump was down in there. So all that water went through that charcoal for a filter. And you also dumped the rain water from your roof in that cistern. And then another thing that was done quite a bit was—in the wintertime—before the ice got too deep and froze, everybody would go and get a bunch of ice and drop it in the cisterns, and you'd be surprised how nice and cold that kept the water all summer.

◆

Ernie Hanna: We were going to make a modern sump. Well, just out in front of the house, we dug a big hole there—oh, I don't know—ten or twelve feet across, and eight or ten feet deep, and then filled it full of big rocks. But we didn't know them days that if we'd piled hay or anything on it first, before we covered it in, it would have made a mat so the dirt wouldn't have soaked down in. And we had a pipe from the kitchen running out for running water. You know, you just wash your hands, and pull the plug, and it would run out into that sump. That worked good for two or three years, but then with rains and stuff, it filled in.

◆

Arnold Molstad: We had a spring that goes into the coolie down somewhere, but isn't welling up enough that it flows. So we'd scrape it out every spring with four horses and a fresno, get her deep enough for a cow to drink out of.

◆

Margaret Pick: The horses and everything drank down at the river. And we had pigs. We got a bunch of pigs. Thought we could make some money on them. And oh, we used to haul water up to those pigs—goodness! Mind you, going down just by our farm—I don't know whether they had made it that way—there was a slope in the bank to the river. We could drive a team down there, and fill up the barrels if we wanted to.

. . . ice

The winter freeze presented its own problems, but also gave the valley people another source of food preservation and income. They chipped river ice for their own ice houses or sold it to the townsfolk.

◆

Ernie Hanna: In the winter, the cattle stayed right there on the frozen river. And then we used to chop holes in the ice for them to drink. Just chop a big round hole part way through the ice, and then just make a small hole in the centre, at the bottom, so the water could come up, so they couldn't fall in or anything like that. Just kind of make a big dish in there, and then just punch one hole through so the water could come up. I don't think we ever had any problems with cattle falling in that way, you know, because you never started feeding them down there until it was froze up solid. But the sides of this dish would get built up with ice around it. The cattle would slobber a little bit, and pretty soon the dish would be sloped up so much that we'd have to chisel that off and cut it down, so's that the cattle could get down to reach the water again.

✦

Margaret Pick: Now another building we had was an ice house.

Gerald Pick: That was away from the house, a little ways, and they had a little shack over top of it.

Margaret Pick: Yeah, it was sort of built down in the hill.

Gerald Pick: Yeah, that was dug in the hill.

Margaret Pick: And we used to cut ice. It was dug down into the hill. We put big blocks of ice in there in the wintertime and covered it with flax straw.

Gerald Pick: Out of the river.

Margaret Pick: On the river. Cut it with an ice saw.

✦

Ernie Hanna: Yeah, we had an ice house. We dug a hole about ten or twelve foot square, about eight feet deep or better. We filled it full of ice in the wintertime. You know, sawed ice and put it there. Then covered it with flax straw. And it would cave in some. It got so that it was caving out about the full size of the building, I guess. We'd have to clean it out and pack more ice in again next year. And it lasted pretty well all summer. And we had a square box built in the middle and set down in there, and we'd kind of cover it. And you could take the milk and cream and stuff that you wanted to keep and set it down in there. Set it on the ice, you know. Then you covered it over. To open it, you'd have to fork the straw and stuff off it, and lift the lid off. But the stuff would remain fresh.

✦

Arnold Molstad: We had an ice house at home. Yeah. We had a hole in the ground and we'd fill it up with ice and pack it with sawdust and then we had a building right over top of it. That kept till pretty well fall. After that, well, you had to take the cream up to the well and hang it from there to cool.

✦

Margaret Pick: We had big hooks to get ahold of the ice and haul it down.

Gerald Pick: And as the winter wore on, the blocks of ice got bigger because they were thicker. I can remember—I think it was about thirty-six inches thick. We'd load four of those blocks of ice on a sleigh and have over two tons, about two and a half or three tons.

Margaret Pick: The ice kept in the ice house a long time. And if we wanted—on Sunday—to have ice cream, made with the old machines, you'd go and take an axe and chop out a chunk of ice and crush it up and make ice cream.

✦

Edgar Sawyer: My brother-in-law dug a kind of a cistern, one time, but it didn't pan out very good, so he used it for an ice house, you know. He'd pump water into it in the winter and it would freeze. And then he'd just build it up. Then in the summer, they'd put their cream and milk and stuff in there, because there was no fridges. But he'd go down there once in a while and chop a little loose and make ice cream, and oh, it was nice. You know, it was handy to the house.

✦

Helen Blondeau: We didn't have no refrigerator in them days. But down where the CPR pump house was, they used to keep ice in there. Because their sheds were made of big logs—big square logs, like they made the dam with. And their sheds were made like that. And then inside this one shed, they'd put ice in there, and then cover it up with straw. So it would stay there until July or August. We'd go and chop big squares of ice, you know. Yeah, of course, that's what they used lots in town, too. Like the Molstads, they used to cut ice and go and bring it to town.

✦

Arnold Molstad: Oh yeah, I cut ice. Got a good price for it. Buck and a quarter a ton—a full load.

Hazel Molstad: All winter he did that.

Arnold Molstad: Yeah, we hauled ice all winter. You put them in—well, it was just like granaries, eh? You put sawdust between the walls and the ice. It kept until the next year. This was in Macoun.

✦

Margaret Pick: Like the Midale creamery—they kept their cream cold with ice in those days, because there was no electricity.

Gerald Pick: I cut all kinds of ice out of that river.

Margaret Pick: After we were married, he hauled for the Midale creamery. Carrying loads, truckloads, of ice. Him and my brother. And it was a heavy load for two men.

Gerald Pick: We had to go down four miles to the river. We'd go down in the morning, cut two big loads of ice and come up and have dinner, and then haul them into Midale, seven miles. Put them in the granary. That's what we spent our winters at.

✦

Edgar Sawyer: Well, we put up ice for the Chinaman here one time and it was three feet square. The chunks that we pulled out. Three of them made a load on a sleigh. We didn't have an ice house on our farm, but they did in town here. Like the hotels and restaurants and that. They had ice houses.

. . . dams and dykes

There were numerous and varied schemes to build dams, dykes, and weirs across the river. Not all were successful, but they became a part of the landscape of the valley and of people's memories of the valley.

✦

Helen Blondeau: There was a nice dam there when it first was built, because I remember when I was real young, I still remember that dam. Because when we went across the river, we had to go on planks about a foot wide. And when we were kids, it was pretty dangerous for us. My mother and dad had to be with us to go across the river and visit our grandmother. She lived across the river.

✦

Jack Muirhead: In the dry years, the biggest problem we had was we figured we could irrigate. And so we bought a pump—four of us. But before we bought the pump, we had to fight like hell to get them to release water out of the Midale dam. To give us some water to irrigate with. And we had a meeting in Midale and I couldn't believe it. I think it was the secretary of the RM up there, he brought it up that they were going to let all this water out, and what's going to happen to the fish. And

There were a number of dams and dykes, such as this one, across the Souris River and crossing them could be a tricky undertaking, especially for children. *Courtesy Helen Blondeau, Midale*

I guess I hit the roof. I was mad! I said, "You put fish before people's livelihood?" Exactly what he was doing. Tourists, you know. I said, "Tourists, my eye! Why don't you look after the people that are here?" So they did. They gave us one thousand acre feet of water. We grew hay. But it seemed every time that we wanted any water from up there, we had to fight for it.

Well, it was flood irrigation, you see, on those flats—and they're very flat. Anyway, four of us bought this pump. We pumped and we irrigated quite a bit with that, and we worked together there, too, with that.

Old railroad ties, such as these being sawed up at the Hanna Ranch in 1929, were hauled home and used for firewood or in the construction of other buildings. *Courtesy Clara Ziehl, Midale*

... fuel

Finding enough fuel was a continuous problem for people in the valley. Different families burned different kinds of fuel in their stoves, depending upon what was available and what they could afford. As mentioned above, coal was the most common fuel, but some families relied on wood, or, occasionally, more exotic materials.

✦

Ernie Hanna: But we burned wood pretty much strictly all day, and we'd always try to have some coal—soft coal, or sometimes you'd get a little hard coal—to bank the fire with at night. Because

boy, that old house—I don't know—it was cold! You would bank the fire at night when it was cold. But the next morning the water in the tea kettle would be froze so the bottom of it would be bulged out, rocking around. And the cat would get up there and set beside it. There was a little bit of warmth in the metal, yet.

We'd pick up railroad ties for firewood all through from Elswick down to the road there where you come down over that crooked hill—we always called it Monson Hill—and all along our property. Why, we'd get all the ties. But we'd have to plough fireguard along there. You know, to protect from fire. So we'd plough a fireguard along the tracks. Well, sometimes you didn't have to do too much because of the lake—a couple of lakes there—which were natural fireguards. If a fire burnt, it would just burn down to the water. Yeah, as long as we kept that fireguard fair along there, we could have all the old ties off it.

✦

Uncle Ernie Hanna: I hauled my coal from Estevan with horses. Down where I lived—I was down south of the river here—and I had to haul all my coal in the fall from Estevan with the horses. And I put in about sixteen to eighteen tons of coal to do me over the winter and summer. I always had to have enough for the summer months, too. Well, I didn't need as much coal in the summer, because I have a big grove around my place, and I always had a lot of waste timber and trees and stuff that I burnt. Sawed it off in the summer months. And then we got a little gas-burner stove for cooking on.

✦

Clara Ziehl: We used mostly wood. We had some coal, but not very much. It was so far to haul the coal, you know. So we used to cut wood in the summertime and in the fall—like we'd use hired help. And they used to pile it up and pile it up.

✦

Carl Hauglum: We hauled a lot of coal by wagon, too. A day up and a day back. Because we were only about thirty miles from Estevan.

Margaret Hauglum: My brothers from Halbrite—I lived in Halbrite—and my brothers used to do the same. Drive horses. And they'd come down to Midale—and we had an uncle who lived here—and they'd stay overnight here, and continue on the next day, and do the same coming back.

Carl Hauglum: Well, people from Yellowgrass hauled coal—that's a long ways out. Lang and Yellowgrass, north here. Because Estevan's the only place there's coal. This coal, you know, they'd ship it, and then it cost you extra money. Freight and stuff. Saves the freight price, you see, hauling your own. We'd haul two tons, two and a half tons. Depends on what kind of a box you had on the wagon.

✦

Jack Boyer: We tried to get as much coal in as we could in the fall. And then a while toward the winter, you'd have to go get some more. But we had room for quite a lot of coal. We'd have to use about twenty, twenty-five, thirty tons. We had a kind of a shed for it. You have to have a shed for it, because you couldn't leave it outside, you know. You have to have it covered up, or it would just all slag up.

✦

Duncan Boyer: Now we three boys, Wilfred, Jack, and I were able to haul coal from the Estevan mines. This always seemed to take place in the coldest weather and we often had to wait in line with others to get our coal. We used a team and wagon, or sleigh, whichever was necessary. Most of the time we walked behind our vehicle to keep ourselves warm. It seems there were no warm parkas and fur-lined boots at that time, and we had at least eighteen miles to travel one way. (excerpt from *Memories*)

Carl Hauglum: Some farmers in the valley had little coal mines. That's a lot of hard work to get that little coal. They could get only a two- or three-foot seam in the ground. Dangerous, you know. You had to haul a lot of dirt to get at the coal. And it wasn't really good coal either—slagged up pretty bad. But people weren't scared to work them days. They wouldn't do it now. Young people won't.

◆

Margaret Pick: Yeah, the Ziehls. He was very small. We used to watch him—us kids. He would start a hole right down at the bottom of the side hill. And he'd dig and fill a bag of dirt and back out— pull it out. And bring another bag full of dirt and pull it out, until he got into the coal seam. And how in the world he ever done it, I don't know. Him and old Ralph Gravell—he used to come down. He was from Goodwater. They were friends and grew up together. And he'd

come down and dug a hole like that. It's hard to believe. And they picked that coal and put it in a bag, and then backed out of the hole and pulled the bag back out. It was just a hole big enough for them to get in and work.

◆

Esther Hanna: Every place my father went, he dug in. Every place he thought he'd find coal, you know.

Ernie Hanna: No. Five or six brothers. Her folks' house was down across the flat near the river. And they came up over the hill and down by the river farther, and they dug back in there. They had quite a big mine, where they could walk in. And they went at quite an angle down back in there—oh, I don't know—a hundred feet or so before they hit the coal. They had a pretty good seam of coal there, too, but then just about that time, they folded up and quit. I mean of course there was no road to even get in with a team and wagon hardly, you know.

My wife's dad knew where every seam was. He was always mining and he could kind of tell by the little coal dust come out of here or there where a gopher dug a hole. So he went pretty much by that, you know. Because places where he had the coal in the side hill, he wouldn't get more than maybe two or three or four or five feet in till he'd be hitting the little seam of coal which would spread out and get deeper. And it was more like hard coal than soft coal. Yeah, and the seam wouldn't be any more than a foot or two wide. You'd just crawl in there and have to take it out, with a clay base over top and underneath.

Esther Hanna: My dad wasn't a very big person. He was short.

Ernie Hanna: You done everything by laying down. And you'd shovel and throw it into a kind of an old tin thing, and then get outside and take a rope and pull it out. Then you'd just crawled back in. I've thought of it since—different times—you crawl back quite a long ways. You had to dig without a brace or anything.

I'd still like to have his old pick that he had. He kept that thing so sharp that it was just about like a needle point on both ends. Just a little light miner's pick.

Young Etta McDonald went with her father to get two loads of coal one day. They mined their own and had one load on at noon when they stopped to sit in the hole while they ate their frozen sandwiches. They had just crawled out of the hole when it caved in and Mr. McDonald simply looked at his daughter and said, "God, Etta, that was a close shave." (excerpt from *Recollections of the Past*)

Coal provided another important source of fuel in the valley. Early settlers at this homestead (possibly the Hess farm, SE 1/4 24-5-13 W2) discovered a coal seam, seen here as a dark band. The archaeological team found a number of such holes dug into hillsides, especially in the Roughbark–Jewel Creek area of the Souris Valley. Instead of making the long trip to Estevan for coal, settlers often found their own sources. *Courtesy Western Heritage Services, Saskatoon*

Carl Hauglum: Cow chips. You've heard about that? In the summertime? I can remember that.

Margaret Hauglum: His mother used to go out and have to pick cow chips.

Carl Hauglum: Yeah, my mother did. She picked them up. Carried a gunny sack and filled it up. It made a good fire. Oh, it would burn like heck. You know, they're dried out. It's all hay, you know—straw. Oh, they had to be dry. You think you could cook on that stuff? A lot of people now would say, "Ugh! Eek!"

Margaret Hauglum: Well, there's nothing to it when you pick it up out in the pasture.

Carl Hauglum: It's light. Cow pies, they call them.

Margaret Hauglum: They burned good— light and airy.

◆

Ernie Hanna: My wife went up to visit neighbours. They were using chunks of old rubber inner tubes from tires for fire, you know. And she figured, "Man, you know, that really gives heat." So she was cooking something, and she poked in a whole bunch of rubber and the whole stove got red hot and the stove pipes were red hot. And she used the washboard and one thing and another—she stuck that between the wall and the stove, and everything she could think of to save the house from burning. So it burnt the plaster up—it was all lath and plaster, you know. She took the ashes out of the bottom and dumped it on top of it to try to smother it. But I mean, that rubber, when you get it burning, there was not much smothering or putting it out.

. . . ash

Whatever was burned for fuel, the result was ash. Again, different people got rid of their ashes in different ways—some simply hauled them out to an ash pile, while others recycled their ash.

◆

Margaret Pick: Ashes from the stove went on the road, because they'd pack. And also Mom used to use ashes when she was planting a garden. Ashes are good to keep those cutworms out of the garden. She used to put ashes in the row before she'd plant. And also I think she threw a lot of ashes on the garden. Just throw them on.

Gerald Pick: When everybody was burning coal in the wintertime, the ashes were generally put outside until they were out. And then hauled in barns to fill holes, because you know them ashes will pack like cement.

Wayne Pick: Our driveway here is all coal ash.

Gerald Pick: But everybody did that because of the dirt. You know, with dirt floors in barns, you get holes. That's where your ashes got.

◆

Hazel Molstad: You had an ash pile. And then you get a whole bunch, and then you used the ashes to fill in in the barn, a bit back of the cows.

Arnold Molstad: That stuff is just like cement.

Hazel Molstad: If that ever got hard, you never had to worry about it breaking off or anything.

Arnold Molstad: Yeah, any holes there were around the barnyard, you'd just dump it in there.

◆

Jack Boyer: I remember at one time you'd take the ashes and spread them out on the road. In the spring of the year, have a big pile of ashes. Take them out and spread them on the road—right on the road.

Recycled ashes were useful for everything from keeping cutworms out of the garden to filling in holes in the barn floor. Trash burning barrels were used to get rid of what little garbage there was. Pete Molstad homestead (NE 1/4 25-3-11 W2). *Courtesy Western Heritage Services, Saskatoon*

Food

It's not surprising that so many memories of life in the valley are about food. Almost everyone was concerned with raising or growing food, and making sure that the family was well-fed was the top priority of the subsistence farmer. Although store-bought food made up a part of the valley family's diet, most survived on what they could raise themselves.

✦

Clara Ziehl: Mom would probably go to the store to buy some peas and beans, if she were out. But she bought very few things.

... three meals a day

Except during threshing, there were three meals a day in the valley home: breakfast, dinner, and supper. Each was a substantial meal, since working outdoors from early morning to the last light of day burned a lot of calories.

✦

Edgar Sawyer: Start at breakfast? Well, you have oatmeal. Wasn't so much of toast, because we didn't have a toaster. You had a little rack thing to hold four slices of bread. Put it over the coals of the

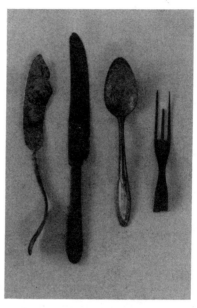

It took a number of homestead digs before an entire set of cutlery was collected. It is very rare to find a complete set on one farm. Spoon and knife from Klyne/Blondeau homestead (SW 1/4 30-3-10 W2); fork from Sawvell farm (NE 1/4 18-5-12 W2); butter knife from Hinzman farm (SW 1/4 7-3-9 W2). *Courtesy Western Heritage Services, Saskatoon*

stove—coal stove. And then you'd have eggs, and you'd have potatoes or pancakes. It wasn't a cup of coffee and a cigarette, I tell you. Because you worked about two hours before you got in there to get breakfast. And then at dinnertime it was meat and potatoes. And eggs—you had all you wanted of them, you know. There wasn't no such thing as one egg. Fry them and boil them and scramble them. We used to hard-boil them and take the yolk out and mix that with mustard or something. Made a dressing and put it back in.

✦

Gerald Pick: At home on the farm it was generally, like, warmed-up fried potatoes and eggs.
Margaret Pick: We used to eat—even after we were married—we would always make a meal out of eggs, rather than meat. One meal a day was eggs of some kind. Fried or boiled. Scrambled.

✦

Edgar Sawyer: And lots of chickens. We raised them, too, you know. Get an old clucking hen and set her. We used to take her upstairs in the barn. Take them upstairs, you know. You maybe have a dozen of them setting in apple boxes. And then each hen had her box to sit on, you know. And when they hatched them out, then you had a little chicken coop out in the yard. You took them out there and you put that old clucker in the chicken coop, and the little ones running around, you know. Oh, there was lots of work connected with that. The chicken coop was a lean-to on the barn. Then the chickens used to come out of there and go in the horse barn and get in the manger, and then they'd lay eggs in there. And the horses come in, and they liked the eggs, too! If

Ma didn't get there before the horses got there, you'd didn't get many eggs.

✦

Margaret Pick: But like cottage cheese—Mom made her own cottage cheese.
Gerald Pick: Well, everybody did that.
Margaret Pick: Made her own cottage cheese and butter.

✦

Helen Blondeau: Oh yeah, we had a cream separator all the time. And Dad, he used to like this—you soured the milk and then dip curds in whey. Something like what you'd buy in the stores, like cottage cheese. And he always liked that, so he'd always have a pan of milk being soured, and then he'd put it on the stove where it's light—not to burn it. And you'd get your cottage cheese.

✦

Ernie Hanna: Your milk and cream and stuff, you'd just take it and hang it on a rope down right next to the water in the well.

✦

Margaret Pick: We were milking cows, and we hung the cream cans down the well. I often wonder. I was pregnant. My husband was away working. You go there and stand over that well and bring that cream can up, dump your cream in it and let it back down again. A lot of women done that—and how more women didn't go head-first into

that bucket! Because the wells weren't like they are now. You took the lid off and there the hole was. I still hate those wells. It was a hole in the ground. You could have fell in, sure. What was it? About—
Gerald Pick: —twenty feet.

✦

Jack Boyer: We'd make pancakes or bannock or some damn thing.

✦

Marceline Lajimodiere: They were all main meals. For breakfast, we had porridge and we had eggs and we had butter in those days. But we didn't have any bacon, because nobody wanted it. And for dinner we had soup and we had meat, potatoes, vegetables, dessert. There was always a dessert. And supper the same way.

✦

Jack Boyer: Well, it depends on what you're doing, you know. If you're batching out someplace, making your own meals, you have to buy your bread and your meat. Generally have your own potatoes. That was about the main food. You'd have to get your bread and fresh meat in the summertime. Of course, in the wintertime you had all that stuff anyway. Butcher in the fall. Butcher a steer. We didn't have deep freezes at that time. But then you'd have to buy your meats—cold meats.

✦

Cream cans were a common sight on the farm. Many families raised cattle so milk, cream, and butter were usually plentiful. Today you are more likely to see an old cream can in a craft shop with a nostalgic prairie scene painted on it. Klyne/Blondeau homestead (SW 1/4 30-3-10 W2). *Courtesy Western Heritage Services, Saskatoon*

Arnold Molstad: What did we get when we took our wheat to town for flour?
Hazel Molstad: Well then, you'd get your flour and you'd get your bran, you know.
Arnold Molstad: And your breakfast food.
Hazel Molstad: That wasn't bad. And then you'd get cracked wheat, too, I think some.

◆

Uncle Ernie Hanna: Oh, dinner, supper, breakfast. Breakfast, they'd have oatmeal if they want it. Most of them, they didn't. They wanted their meat and potatoes. The cold weather and the work, you know. So they wanted a good meal.

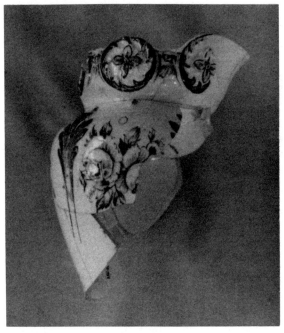

Not all utensils served functional purposes only. This detail from an ornate cream pitcher came from the Klyne/Blondeau homestead (SW 1/4 30–3–10 W2). *Courtesy Western Heritage Services, Saskatoon*

◆

Marceline Lajimodiere: You see, the kids need porridge. Something to hold them up, you know. Not corn flakes. That's just like wind. And some people say, "Well, my kids get corn flakes." I used to make porridge and I used to give them each a boiled egg, once in a while. I didn't want them to get tired of eggs. I never give them any more than one egg. And sometimes I'd make pancakes. And I always fixed their lunches—lunch pails.

◆

Helen Blondeau: Dinnertime was at noon. Yeah, we'd have either pork chops or roasts or potatoes and vegetables and things. Pie, we'd have lots of pie. When the saskatoons came out, we'd make pie. If the rhubarb came out, we made pie. There was lots of that.

◆

Clara Ziehl: Supper was pretty much the same. Your well-boiled potatoes and meat. It wasn't like now—if you have one meal a day, that's all, you know. You never think of having two big meals a day. But yet nobody got fat and nobody had cholesterol. I guess you were working so hard, you didn't have time to get fat.

◆

Margaret Pick: Supper was always meat, potatoes, and vegetables. And we made a lot of puddings at that time because we had milk. We made pies.
Gerald Pick: There was pies.
Margaret and Gerald Pick: Apple.
Margaret Pick: Cream pies. We had rhubarb. Mom used to can rhubarb. And there was some wild strawberries. Very few, but there was sometimes, that she got hold of.

Controlling the temperature in a cookstove could be a challenge, but this did not stop the women from making pies and cakes that make their husbands' mouths water years later as they recall how good they tasted. These cast-iron cookstove parts were found at the Reddemann farm (SE 1/4 7-3-9 W2). *Courtesy Western Heritage Services, Saskatoon*

✦

Ernie Boyer: We had coal and wood stoves. The women had a harder time to control the heat than they do now. But you know those people, they got to so they knew exactly how their stoves worked. They could make pie that's— you don't see that kind of pie nowadays! Yeah, they knew how to make pie, or cake, and it really tasted good. Now I never hardly can buy a pie or cake that tastes like that.

✦

Clara Ziehl: Oh yeah. And cake. I don't think Mom ever made a lot of cookies ahead of time like they would nowadays. But she used to come in and she'd whip up a white cake and put this whipped cream on. We always had lots to eat. Cream, cream, cream. We never had no cholesterol them days either like they do now. I'm telling you. Mom used to come in and stir up the cake with sweet cream. Put it in the oven. And then she'd put whipped cream on top. And just barely get it out of the oven in time for the men.

. . . bread and meat

Most of the women baked their own bread.

◆

Carl Hauglum: One thing—you talk about that now—there wasn't any bakeries around here. Stores didn't handle bread in the early days. Old bachelors had to go to the married people and buy their bread from the farmers. You heard a lot of that.

Margaret Hauglum: Oh no, there was no bakeries here.

Carl Hauglum: That's for sure. Sometimes the homemade bread was better than the boughten anyway. Because you get good home bread-bakers. With practice you learn, I guess.

◆

Helen Blondeau: We made our own bread. I'd have to use about two hundred pounds of flour a month when we were all at home. I used to bake bread twice a week.

◆

Edgar Sawyer: Make baking powder biscuits, you know. We ate a lot of them. Because you make them in no time flat. They don't have to raise or nothing, you see. I made them once. I didn't know how long you cooked them, so I put them in and made sure they were done. God, you couldn't cut them with an axe, by God! I never tried baking them myself a second

The remains of a Blue Ribbon Baking Powder tin from the Hanna Ranch. Baking powder biscuits were fast and easy to make, even if they did not always turn out as planned. *Courtesy Western Heritage Services, Saskatoon*

time. But they were good. I liked them in the mornings with cream of wheat. Oh, we ate a lot of them.

Nobody bought meat. Raising, slaughtering, and preserving one's own meat was a way of life for valley people.

◆

Marceline Lajimodiere: Well, chickens and pigs, cattle. You see, that time there was no deep freezers, no nothing. Well, for the summer, you had to kill something to eat. Rabbits or ducks. And we tried to grow a bunch of chickens, and kill a chicken once in a while. At home we had two big timbers and a crosspiece. And that's where we hung the meat. You have to hang the meat for a night. Like you butcher in the afternoon and leave it hang there till the next day, so the meat goes off before you cut it up. The butchering was done near the barn, close to the barn. Away from the house.

✦

Gerald Pick: Well, there would be a bunch of farmers get together. I know at home, Dad belonged to a beef ring for three or four years. There was an old fellow had a good solid building that he'd butcher in. Well, you take your critter and you go and help him butcher. And he'd cut it up, and then you'd get a different piece of that meat around as far as it went, like the whole summer. And generally once a week you had fresh meat. They were all neighbours, and they tried to get the beef as near the same size to take over there and butcher. It worked out good for fresh meat, because there was no way you could keep it. Nobody could butcher a whole beef and keep it.

✦

Helen Blondeau: Yeah, we used to have a beef ring, too. Every Friday they'd go and kill a beef. This was in Macoun they did that. Or by Macoun, not right in town. Yeah, I remember they used to have those beef rings. They'd butcher on Friday and next Friday they'd butcher again. I guess each farmer would donate a cow. And then we'd have the meat for the week—fresh meat.

✦

Edgar Sawyer: Well, yes, the beef ring worked all right. So many got together and then they butchered every week. But some of them got so, you know, that there was awful long necks and awful long legs on some of them critters.

✦

Ernie Boyer: Different guys would get together to butcher two or three hogs. They didn't do like now. They got together and cooperated. No money. They'd help each other, and maybe a couple of weeks later, my dad would be gone for a day butchering with somebody else.

✦

Margaret Pick: Mom used to butcher a beef, and then she'd put it in the back of the buggy and away she'd go. And she'd sell chunks of it to all the neighbours.

✦

Clara Ziehl: And, of course, Mom used to sell meats. She used to butcher—she'd butcher one day, and cut it up and put it in the democrat and go around with it, you know, and deliver it. And you wonder how in the world she could ever done all that work. And then she used to keep some meat for herself, you know. And then a few days later, she'd butcher another beef, and then she'd do the same thing again. And then usually she used to kill a pork in the spring, and they used to fry that down, you know. She'd fry it and put it in those big jars. The fat would be on top, and she'd put another layer of pork on top of the fat, so you could always go and dig it out. And it used to keep real good that way.

◆

Edgar Sawyer: At that time you had to can your meat, you know. Like then you went through a process of cooking it. The beef, they used to put that in jars. Cooked it and put it in jars. That was pretty good stuff, canned stuff like that. It was nice and tender, too. But you take bacon and pork and that stuff, you know. Some people dry-salted and some put the pork in brine to cure it. It would be so bloody salty, you could hardly eat it. And then tough! After it's been in there for about three months, you know. You could hardly cut it with an axe. You had to put so much salt on it to keep it from spoiling, that—God, it was something! It was what they called parboiled. Put in the frying pan with some water and let it cook for a half an hour before dinner, you know. Then pour that off, and then fry it or cook it. But it was lots of salt, all right. I often wonder how they lived so long, some of them people. God, the first thing the doctor told me when I had a checkup was stay away from salt. No salt and no this and no that. I thought, "My God, what happened in the early days?" They just lived on that, you know.

◆

Margaret Pick: It's remarkable when you think about it. Remember how we used to cure bacon and hang it up in the basement or in the cellar? And bring it up and it would be covered with mould, and we'd take vinegar and wash it off. And then sometimes you'd soak it. And we ate it.

Gerald Pick: Well, it had so much salt in it.

Margaret Pick: We soaked the salt out. And we used to butcher the pork. Fry all the side pork and that down, and then put it in these big crocks and then pour lard over it. It would keep. We kept the crocks in the basement.

◆

Uncle Ernie Hanna: Well, they had what they call a smoke house, and put the meat so long in there before it was cured. It was really good, too. They had it hanging up in the basement rack. You can't have too big a piece of meat for smoking. Well quartered up. Like pork. You could smoke the hind quarter and front quarter. And cut the middle out, of course, and smoke that, too. Boy, does that have a good taste to it!

◆

Margaret Pick: They talk about how you used to cure your bacon. Put it in oats. Shove it in to keep it fresh.

Gerald Pick: Some people did that.

Margaret Pick: We never did.

Wayne Pick: That was a Russian tradition.

Gerald Pick: Yeah.

Wayne Pick: Put it in the granary, in grain.

Gerald Pick: Well, you know, that works. We knew a couple of old bachelors living together, and we used to go there and thresh for them. And they had hams that they buried in the wheat— but they were the only guys in the country that ever had any wheat them years. They put hams in there in the spring and we ate them, threshing. It stayed all summer buried in that grain.

✦

Helen Blondeau: We didn't can much. No, we just salted it. And we'd have a smoke house and make bacon and ham. Yeah, it was just a little building where we'd smoke and hang our meat. And we'd try and find some hard wood to smoke it. It would taste just like the ham you eat today, only it was a little saltier. I guess they used to have to put a lot of salt in it to keep it, them days.

✦

Margaret Pick: I was pregnant once. Fried down all that pork. If you think a person can't get sick! Oh! And then beef—we used to cut it up in little pieces and sometimes brown it and put it in sealers and then process it. Put it in a sealer and can it, same as you can fruit now. Boil it three hours in the canner and then bring it out. And we made stew.

✦

Clara Ziehl: Oh, I used to like canned beef. I'd like to have some canned beef right now. It was really good, you know. Mom just cut it up in chunks and put it in a sealer and put salt and pepper on it. Put it in the boiler for three hours. And that's all. That's all there is to it. And it kept for years and years. I'd sure like to have some again. Because it made nice gravy, you know. The liquid would come up over halfway on the sealer, you know. And, of course, when you took it out of the jars, you just take this out and heat it up and put some onion in it. It was really good. Yeah. You don't dare put water on it. The beef made its own juice.

✦

Arnold Molstad: Oh, we canned meat.

Hazel Molstad: We used to can meat. Well, there was no power, no freezers in here when we came. You sterilize your sealers and cut your meat—put them up. Salt and pepper in it and seal them up and put them on the stove and boiled them for three hours.

Arnold Molstad: And you know that was better-tasting meat than you get out of the fridge. I sure missed that when she quit doing that.

Hazel Molstad: Well, it was handy. Now if somebody drops in, your meat's froze solid—it takes a little longer now to make a meal. You'd can meat about once a year. And it was good. You could make hamburgers or you brown the meat a little, and you put them in your jars with a little liquid on it.

✦

Carl Hauglum: Canned meat. Didn't have a fridge. It was good, too, that home-canned stuff. Cold meat got the old jelly on it, you know. That jelly's as good as the meat.

Margaret Hauglum: Canned chicken. Yeah, we smoked hams and bacons. And in order to keep the flies away—after they were smoked or salted—we'd bury them in the bin of oats or wheat.

Carl Hauglum: Dry curing.

Margaret Hauglum: It keeps the flies away, you know. Of course you wrapped it up first a little bit with cheesecloth.

Carl Hauglum: That's what the Indians do yet, don't they? They smoked meat at the camps—fish and that. They keep the bugs away, I suppose. I like smoked stuff, myself.

Margaret Hauglum: We smoked meat in a snowbank one year. Just in a hole in a big high snowbank. Made a fire and hung the meat up in the snow.

Carl Hauglum: Worked out all right. Put a lid on top, you know.

◆

John Dowhanuik: The old sow—we butchered it for the winter, and that was our meat. We butchered it and burnt the hair off of it with straw. We never scalded a pig in them days—we didn't know nothing. Butchering a pig was kind of a big do, you know—just like a celebration. Hit it in the head with a hammer and bleed it. Mother kept the blood and made sausage, and with some of the blood she would prepare what the Scotchmen called a haggis: she would take the liver and the heart and the skin of the feet and the skin of the head, and you ground all that up in a coarse grinder. Then you mix it up with the blood and put it in the pig's stomach—though she didn't do that very much. She used to put the mixture in a ten-pound sugar sack—instead of cleaning out the pig's stomach—and boiled the sack. And after it was boiled, you took it out and pressed all the water out. And you just cut it up, just like cheese, you know. You eat it that way. Something like the Scotchmen make haggis.

◆

Margaret Pick: Uncle Henry used to trap beaver and skin them. Stretch them.

Wayne Pick: Uncle Henry did use the tail.

Margaret Pick: We never did.

Wayne Pick: Uncle Henry used to make soup out of that.

Margaret Pick: Yeah, beaver-tail soup. Two old guys in Midale—every time he came in with a beaver, they were there to get that tail. Another thing we ate a lot of was wild pheasants and prairie chickens. On Saturday, we'd go to town. When we lived down on the ranch, we'd hitch up the team and the buggy and we'd go. And Gerry would maybe shoot once at a pheasant and I'd shoot. We'd go home and pick them and have a Sunday dinner.

◆

Ernie Boyer: There were grouse. They call

them ruffled grouse. They're native to this country, but the Hungarian partridge were brought in from someplace else, and so were the pheasants. We didn't know nothing about those when I was young.

◆

Jack Boyer: Yeah, a lot of prairie chickens, at one time. But then when the pheasants were introduced, they done quite well for a long time. Then the hard winters came. Oh boy, I remember we were down in the valley one winter in 1947, and after the big storm—a very early storm—there were about a hundred of them pheasants out in the field just south of the river there, laying in the snow, dead. Seemed a shame.

◆

Clara Ziehl: We used to eat lots of ducks. And my dad used to eat ducks—I'm telling you—he bought Mom a big roaster. I've got it yet. A big aluminum roaster you put five ducks in, side by side. And they used to pick them ducks. And she used to pick them and save the feathers. That's just one more thing she did. They used to go out and hunt, you know, and bring these ducks home, and they were good to eat, you know.

◆

Arnold Molstad: You ever work with turkeys? Boy, you need earplugs. My wife had a hundred of them in the building out there. You couldn't even think!

◆

Carl Hauglum: We used to raise live turkeys, too. That was our income for the year. Hundreds of turkeys every year. And by Christmas time, there was a lot of Christmas parcels and clothes.

Margaret Hauglum: That was a big job.

Carl Hauglum: For five dollars you could buy stuff, too, in them days. A lot of stuff, you know. Yeah, a big job picking—cleaning and picking.

Margaret Hauglum: The men would kill the turkeys in the barn, and then you'd pick them in the barn, and you'd bring them in the house—

Carl Hauglum: —pin feathers—

Margaret Hauglum: —and the women would finish picking the pin feathers, and sometimes these darn turkeys would hardly be dead yet. If they were struck right, the feathers would come out really easily.

Carl Hauglum: Well, you see you got the right equipment and the right temperature. I suppose they can't do it like in the cities, where they got those big tumblers that take the feathers off. That saved money—that cost money, too, you see.

Margaret Hauglum: We had to wash the turkeys by hand.

Carl Hauglum: Did your own work, even if it was two bits a turkey—I suppose that was twenty-five dollars for one hundred, so you save your own money.

Margaret Hauglum: Then you had to wash the head. You had to wash that stinky head and the stinky feet.

Carl Hauglum: Had to wrap them.

Margaret Hauglum: Yeah, you sold them like they were, you know.

Carl Hauglum: They want them that way with the head and everything—the feet and head.

    To kill them, you only had to stick them under the tongue with a sharp knife. I did a lot of that. Cut the blood vessel under their tongue close to the throat. I used a small blade, less than a quarter-inch. A sticking knife. Sharp little blade.

Margaret Hauglum: A real sharp one.

✦

Gerald Pick: There was the man that brought a bear into the country. He went up to buy some horses, and wherever he bought them horses, they had this cub bear they gave him. And he had it for a while, but it got half-mean. So finally the butcher in Midale butchered it and sold bear meat. So people got their first taste of bear.

. . . and fish

The Souris River was always a source of fish—summer and winter.

✦

Margaret Pick: Let's not get on to fish! My mom used to—up the river quite a little ways up towards Monson's Grove, there was a place there where the water never was too deep, except if it really flooded. And she made a dam across with rocks and so. The fish would come in there, and then she'd catch them, eh? And then she would clean them, and we ate canned fish, smoked fish, fresh fish, salted fish.

Wayne Pick: She won't even eat a fresh fish out of the water now.

Margaret Pick: I just cannot eat fish! All those little suckers and pickerel. In the spring, she used to catch hundreds of them.

✦

Clara Ziehl: We used to catch fish, and then Mom used to salt them and smoke them. They were sure good. I can remember how she used to do it—when you had them all salted and hung up. They'd keep forever like that. And then she used to put them on the frying pan and put cream on and fry them that quick—cook them that way, you know. They were rich, but they were sure good.

✦

Jack Muirhead: To get back to that story that I was going to tell you about. They let the water down from Midale dam in the winter. Now I don't know what—whether they figured there was going to be a flood or what. But anyway, they let the water out in February, and I looked out the window one day, and here comes this water down the river, you know. Snowbanks just like waves, you know—snowbanks in the winter. This water was coming down and over the top of these banks. Here's all these fish. Oh, my God! So my neighbour and I—we went out with two pitchforks, one each—and we threw them on the bank. Well, most of them were mullet or suckers, you know. They were big, too. Fat fish. And I suppose we threw about forty or fifty of them out on the bank. And there was about six or eight jackfish. And of course we didn't think anything about the mullets. That was in the morning. In the afternoon, I went to town and then come home, and here my wife is, canning all these damn fish. I don't know how many sealers! But she wasn't satisfied just to can them. She had to take beet juice to make it look like salmon. They were good. You know, out of that cold, cold water like that?

Joyce Muirhead: I made them into salmon with beet juice. If you use vinegar, it dissolves all the bones. You know, those things are full of bones, and you can't eat them. But that was good salmon. Beet juice to make it pink. It looked just like pink salmon, and it tasted good.

Jack Muirhead: So I ate fish about every way you could. She made I don't know how many different kinds of dishes out of that stuff.

Joyce Muirhead: Because that's all we ate, because that was the year our pig ran away. Yeah, at least we ate. We had fish cakes and fish loaf and fish— it's a wonder I eat fish at all to this day. And I still like it.

◆

Gerald Pick: You know, you're getting back to them fish days. Well, there was

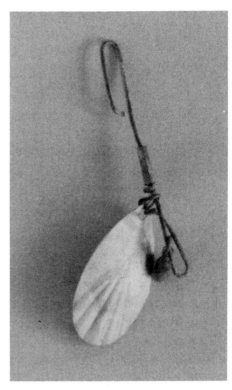

Canned, smoked, fresh, or salted—fish were a constant in the diet of the valley settlers, and fishing was a popular diversion for the children, when they could find the time. Fish lure from the Klyne/Blondeau homestead (SW 1/4 30-3-10 W2). *Courtesy Western Heritage Services, Saskatoon*

all these suckers, and my uncle's brother, he used to be a great fisherman, and he'd go around and sell these. Well, go and selling suckers, you know—nobody seemed to want to buy them. So he gets himself a book— they're not really a sucker, you know. They're "tullibee." Tullibee was these little fish. So he'd go and ask people if they wanted to buy tullibee. Sure, they'd all buy some, a bunch of them. But they were all the same fish as what we called suckers, but by a new name. And everybody bought them.

... fruits and vegetables

Gardens provided most of the vegetables for the valley family. Berries, either wild or domestic, were the main fruit, although it was quite common for people to buy apples and dried fruit in the stores in town.

✦

Margaret Hauglum: And of course with having a big garden, you have to do your canning, preserve your vegetables. Well, peas and beans. Beet pickles. And of course there was no pressure cookers, and you'd put your vegetables in jars and you'd boil them for three hours on the stove in the boiler.

✦

Helen Blondeau: We never had no root cellar. We just had our cellar under our house, just a dirt cellar. But the vegetables all kept there—it seemed like they kept better than what they keep now. It would stay cool, and the potatoes would keep good and the other vegetables, like carrots and turnips. And I know we'd have a lot of cabbage. Dad liked cabbage. We'd sometimes make sauerkraut.

✦

John Dowhanuik: We always had a big garden. Always planted everything that we could think of, whether we could use it or not. Potatoes, cucumbers, cabbage to make sauerkraut, and maybe some turnips. Of course, we never ate the turnips—we fed them to the pigs. Onions, garlic, a few carrots—we ate them raw. In them days we didn't prepare the vegetables like you do now. We never heard of tomatoes. We planted corn. Stuff that you could eat right away. Mom never canned nothing—she didn't know how to can. Except she made beet pickles. But the pickles—you don't can them. Forty-five jars of pickles, forty-five jars of sauerkraut, for the winter. It had to be kept in the house until it fermented, and then we took it out to the granary where it was froze. And if you wanted some, you'd go out there and chop it out from the grain. And that's the way that we kept it.

✦

Uncle Ernie Hanna: Buy fruit from the store. Fruit was shipped in like that. Pretty reasonable. And they take it home and can it. All they could take, because they didn't get to town every time. Well now, fresh fruit—they wanted it so much. They'd buy it and can it.

✦

Edgar Sawyer: Oh yeah, they come in the store in boxes, you know, the same as they do now. Go in and buy a box of apples. Dad—when he come from down east there, you know—he had apples right off the farm down there. All they wanted. Different kinds. And he used

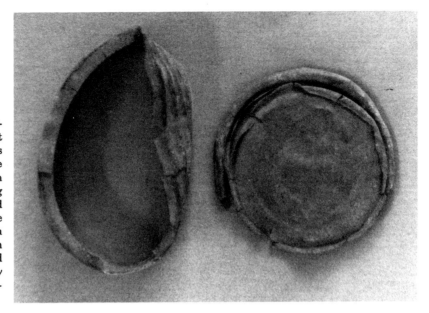

Most families had a huge garden and either picked wild fruit or bought fruit such as apples to make preserves. But the women canned more than fruits and vegetables during the busy fall season. Meat and fish were also "put up" for the winter. Sealer ring from Hanna Ranch, canning jar lid from Klyne/Blondeau homestead (SW 1/4 30-3-10 W2). *Courtesy Western Heritage Services, Saskatoon*

to buy a dozen boxes of apples here, you know. Put them down in the cellar in the fall of the year, and we had apples to do all winter. You'd have apple pie and apple sauce. Make different things, you know.

✦

Bella Gardipie: Mom used to buy fruit in the fall—peaches and plums and pears. They were in the stores then. I remember them bringing fruit home by the case, and she'd can them. Mom used to do it in an open kettle, in a big kettle. She used to put the fruit in and put the sugar in and boil it. Put them in sterilized jars.

✦

Margaret Pick: We used to have oranges and apples in school.

Gerald Pick: There was quite a bit of fruit. We had apples—that was one thing. Because generally I think 90 percent of the farmers in the fall, they take a load of grain to town, and come back with four or five boxes of apples—and that sleigh would be pretty near loaded. Hundred pounds of oatmeal.

Margaret Pick: One hundred pounds of flour.

Gerald Pick: And that was all brought home and stored.

✦

Ernie Boyer: Any place along the river fruit was plentiful. If it wasn't along the river bank, it was along the side hills. Patches here and there. A lot of saskatoons along the side of the hills. If you see trees, that's probably saskatoon or chokecherry trees.

✦

John Dowhanuik: In them days there was lots of chokecherries in the ravine south of our place. In the days when there were berries down there, you could go down there and pick berries, and you know, there'd be fifty or sixty people down there from all over, picking berries.

✦

Bella Gardipie: We always picked berries. Saskatoons—we used to can a lot of saskatoons. There used to be a patch of raspberries up there on the side of the hill. I remember picking that. Across the river from home, right beside the hill, we used to pick all the berries there. There was a kind of a ravine there and there was saskatoons and chokecherries there. I remember picking about a pailful in there. And that's where we used to pick raspberries, too.

✦

Clara Ziehl: But there was lots of saskatoons, gooseberries, raspberries, along the river, you know. Mom used to pick them. She used to can hundreds of quarts every year.

✦

Helen Blondeau: Grandma grew raspberries. She had raspberries and gooseberries, I remember. Yeah, she'd grow them right along the river. There was saskatoons, too. The saskatoons were easy to can, because you didn't need much sugar for them. We'd dry some, if we got too many. We'd put them on a clean sheet and then put some of this cheesecloth on top, you know, so the flies wouldn't get on them. You'd have to keep stirring them all the time, because they'd get mouldy. But we'd dry big bags full of them. Then in the winter we'd just soak them and eat them like dried fruit. Yeah, something like raisins. Make pies and use them like raisins. They were so sweet once they were dried, they seemed to keep all their sweetness.

✦

Margaret Pick: And then Mom used to pick saskatoons. Oh, this old Minnie Larson—she lived up by Monson's Grove, and she said Mom used to come at breakfast time already with two great big water pails full of saskatoons she picked. Boy! And then she'd take a boat—gooseberries and black currants, they used to grow right along the river. And she had this old boat, and she used to take it—she'd go up in the boat and pick them in the boat. And then she made jelly and jams—gooseberry jam. I never did like it. And then chokecherries. She used to make chokecherry drink. In fact, I still do. My one son really likes it. Take the chokecherries and grind them—stones and all—through the grinder. And then you cover that pulp with pure vinegar and let it sit for so long. And then you drain it, and then you put it on the stove and boil it with sugar. And you do the same with freshie in it. Put a couple of table-spoons of juice in a glass and then boil it. And that's what we used to drink. And of course chokecherry jelly and pancakes. I still make it. It's a lot like jelly. It's not as thick as jelly, but you pour it over your pancakes.

✦

Clara Ziehl: Jams and jellies and fruit and everything. Mom used to can hundreds of quarts of juneberries, you know. She'd can, oh, probably three hundred quarts of juneberries. I often wonder how Mom ever did all that work.

✦

Margaret Hauglum: When I was a kid, or teen-ager, living in Halbrite there, a bunch of us young girls got together and we had a Bennett buggy and a team of horses, and we drove down to the river west of Halbrite and picked berries.

✦

Marceline Lajimodiere: Well, saskatoons, chokecherries. They used to dry saska-toons for winter. And they used to make a dish where they used to render beef fat, or something like that. And they used to mix that with saskatoons with a little bit of sugar. And that made pemmican. I had to make it to find the berries. Looking for berries. Good. Yeah—that and bannock. Oh, that used to taste good.

... drink

The valley people were self-sufficient in almost all ways—even in their drinking habits. They preferred home-brewed beer, wine, and spirits to whatever was available in town, and no one thought too much about the legalities involved.

Not all of the beverages consumed were of the strictly legal kind, and if you look hard enough, who knows? there may be a few of these jugs left intact under the ground on the odd homestead. Just be careful when you remove the cork! *Courtesy Western Heritage Services, Saskatoon*

✦

Margaret Pick: Mom used to make home-made beer. Then of course she bought the hops. Once Dad was out working and he was going to take the top off a jug which was sitting on the wagon, you know. And the stopper flew up and hit him in the eye and gave him a black eye. But that stuff, you pretty near had to open into a pitcher. Because as soon as you took the top off, it would all foam, you know. Yeah. Mom used to make homemade beer all the time. Never wine.

✦

Marceline Lajimodiere: Chokecherries. Those are for the people who made wine. They had chokecherry wine. That was easy to make because it fermented so easy, you know. Chokecherry juice.

✦

Helen Blondeau: Well, they used to make wine with chokecherries. Yeah, they'd boil the chokecherries. Then they'd kind of grind it—well, chop it, and then put the yeast in. And it would be good wine. I think they didn't even have a recipe. They just made it like that. Because there was a lot of choke-cherries, too, and you couldn't do much with chokecherries. Oh yeah, we also used to make dandelion wine. Oh, there were lots of dandelions along the roadsides. They're supposed to be good to eat, too, but we never ate them. We just made wine.

✦

Carl Hauglum: There was home-brew in them days. Made a lot of beer and malt whiskey. Brewed home-brew. They made money on that, too, you know. You seen a still and all that? Coils that run through cold water and a cooker.

✦

Uncle Ernie Hanna: I had to go down to a place one time in the wintertime. And I'm cold. A man said, "Aw, just come on in—it's cold." Pretty near knocked my hat off when I opened the door. Had a bottle in there fermenting behind the stove. Made liquor out of wheat. I said, "By gol, good thing you're a long way from the goddamned police here. You'd sure have a ticket." He said, "I know that."

✦

Margaret Pick: I remember one time— I was supposed to go out and have a drink, and this guy had made home-brew. Oh, I'll never forget how that burned my throat. I was seventeen then.

. . . a full lunch pail

The overall impression one gets when listening to these memories is that no one went hungry. Whatever hardships existed, there was always food on the table. Even in the worst years of the Depression, valley people could always find a way of feeding themselves, and in general, they fed themselves well.

✦

Marceline Lajimodiere: Yeah, people lived better in them days than now. Just like my son Harold said to the kids at the community college: "And I told them," he says, one time, "you

know, during the hard times—supposed to be during the thirties—when
we were just maybe in grade four,
grade five, us two. Our lunch pails was
the same as during good times at
school. There was nothing missing."
Well, I baked. I liked to bake. I used to
bake, and then we had our eggs. I'd
make egg sandwiches. And sometimes
we'd buy some baloney. And I used to
bake cookies and cakes and stuff. And
Harold would say, "Our lunch pail was
the same in good times as in hard
times."

Good Times in the Valley

Although life was tough in the valley, there was plenty of time for entertainment. Without radio or television, people made their own fun.

. . . swimming

In warm weather, the children spent a good part of their time (when they weren't doing their chores) swimming.

✦

Joyce Muirhead: The river was kind of muddy. And then it would get low. Or else it was too high. Like it would flood the flats, if they got rain in Yellowgrass in June. Then that valley was just a lake. The kids couldn't swim in the river. But they did swim at MacDonald Lake a bit. That's fed by springs, eh? But it wasn't a good place to swim.

I built them a swimming pool in the backyard, and the kids spent days out there, too. They had a great time out there. Made out of an old steel culvert. A neighbour helped me put a cement bottom in it, and we put a drain in it. And it was just a beautiful pool.

Jack Muirhead: It was what?—about six or seven feet across.

Joyce Muirhead: Yeah, and deep, and it had an edge, you know, where they could step off and get in. Because we have twin daughters, eh? Our babies are twins, and they spent half their lives in that pool. And it was great, because it was hot. We didn't have air conditioning, and it was just like living in hell almost, because we were right on the hill there, and the sun just beat in on you. And these kids just spent all day in the pool. And they had a little boat, a little raft down there. Oh, it was great for kids.

✦

Duane Boyer: During the summer it was great fun to swim in the river. The river was less than six feet deep at the bridge and we endured broken beer bottles, lost fish hooks, bloodsuckers, itchy weeds, and snakes. We loved it. (excerpt from *Memories*)

✦

Margaret Pick: None of us—I think my brother could swim a little, and I think my sister older than I could swim a little. There were six girls and one boy. And we used to—Dad used to go up and swipe new ties from the railroad, when they were putting new ties in.

And I was only six then, five or six, and we used to get on those ties here and would go all away around the bend in the river and come out on the other side of the pasture.

. . . skating and sliding

In the winter, the hills, river, and lakes were perfect for skating and sliding.

◆

Ernie Boyer: We did have a ski slide along the hill. We'd sleigh, or we'd go skating along the river. Sometimes that was our recreation.

◆

Helen Blondeau: And we'd go skating down the river. Yeah, and, oh, we used to have a lot of parties skating. Yeah, we had lots of fun. It seems now they don't have fun like that. I suppose they do in their own way. Well, we had just real skate boots with skates on. Some of the kids had clamps that clamp onto your shoe, but kids didn't like those very much, because they'd take the soles off the shoes. But we all learned to skate. We could skate for miles down the river. And then the boys would go down there and they'd play hockey. And then if there was too much snow, they scraped out a big patch and flooded it. Because they could flood it there, you know, by the CPR pump house. And there they'd make a big skating rink. So in the wintertime we had lots of fun. Yeah. And then there was those hills—going sliding with sleighs. Toboggans. We just made toboggans of some kind. Some of the places, the hills were pretty steep.

◆

Bella Gardipie: We used to have toboggan parties. That was fun, I liked that.

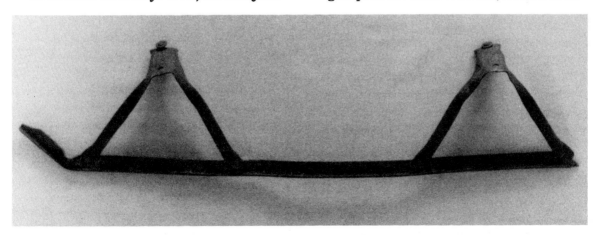

This runner from a child's sled doubtlessly saw its share of good times. The valley was ideal for winter fun (Lajimodiere homestead, NE 1/4 16-3-10 W2). *Courtesy Western Heritage Services, Saskatoon*

Oh gee, there was really good hills in the valley. Up there by Reddemann's, they had a real big one there. If you made it up that hill four times in one night, you were lucky. Yeah, we used to have a lot of fun.

◆

Margaret Pick: Oh, we had lots of good times.
Gerald Pick: House parties.
Margaret Pick: House parties and whist parties and skating. We used to go down on that river, and we would clean the ice off, and then all the neighbours would come and skate. Mom would make cocoa and stuff when we got back. And right up from the house here—or from the barn really—that hill really goes up. North part. And we used to take everything, even a cardboard box, or shovels—scoop shovels—it was always some of them got scoop shovels—older than me. And we'd get up on top of that hill, and we'd come down and across the road and down the river bank. We didn't have sleighs. And we'd go all the way back up again and back down. Cardboard boxes would slide. You'd lay on your stomach hanging on to the end of the cardboard box and you could—oh!

◆

Helen Blondeau: Yeah, there was lots of snow. I remember when I was young, there was a lot of snow. We used to go and dig in the snowbank—great big high snowbank—higher than our heads.

. . . all sorts of fun

The children in the valley always managed to find a way of entertaining themselves, or at least of getting into mischief.

◆

Margaret Pick: Another thing we used to do. My uncle Ernie had four boys. And I can remember they used to have wrestling. And I mean it was wrestling—not this stupid stuff they do now. It was just strength wrestling. Well, I can remember them wrestling.

◆

Bella Gardipie: I will tell about the horrid things we did in school. My big sister Rose was a real stinker. Rose and George LaRocque used to take the horse and buggy and chase Irene McMellon as fast as the horse could go. Imagine how poor Irene had to run. Of course I had to go along, as these stunts took place after school. When I was grown up I couldn't look Irene in the face. Another trick was to drive George as far from his home as we dared without anybody finding out. One day he got too smart. He was standing up driving and using the whip on the horse who was going as fast as he could. The wheel hit a big rock and George went flying. He got up bleeding and crying. He told Mama what happened and Pa found out. We had to walk to school after that. (excerpt from *Memories*)

✦ ✦

Margaret Pick: But we had some beautiful horses. We had some good horses. I remember, I had Miss Fluffie—I called her. Oh, the races. You wonder how we didn't get our necks broken. Race them out as hard as they would go. On the road. There was no gravel then. We used to race. Oh yes. Oh, we raced horses every day we went to school. And I used to get so mad if I didn't have a good horse. Because I was my dad's pet, and I rode horseback long before I ever went to school, I can tell you.

Bella Gardipie: One time Rose started an argument with Arthur LaRocque about whose horse could run faster. Arthur had a big black plough horse, and Rose had our little pony. She insisted I ride with her on the back. Off we went to prove who had the best horse. Well, I fell off and nearly broke my leg. The teacher kept a cold cloth on it all afternoon. I had a big bump on my leg and had to miss school for a while. (excerpt from *Memories*)

The one-room school-house often doubled as a community centre on the Prairies, with Christmas concerts, sports days, and other activities taking place there throughout the year. *Courtesy Helen Blondeau, Macoun*

◆

Gerald Pick: Well, that was one thing—Christmas concerts. They were a big thing. And the schools seemed to have them at different times.

Margaret Pick: So you could go to more than one.

Gerald Pick: That was the only time you didn't have to fight too much to get the team of horses out of the barn. If you were going to the Christmas concert: "You go ahead, but be sure you get blankets on the horses, if you don't get them in the barn."

Margaret Pick: The barn was never big enough.

Gerald Pick: They'd only last two or three hours, but we'd drive fifteen, twenty miles to a school concert. Dad never seemed to mind that.

Margaret Pick: And they used to have some real good plays. Each person had their part and we'd study and we'd practise. Everybody came to Christmas concerts.

Gerald Pick: Especially the parents of the kids. When we were in the school plays, well, Mother and Dad used to always go.

Margaret Pick: And we had what they call field days. Now they call them sports days. In the summertime, when you would go and all compete for racing and jumping at the school grounds. And I was a good sports person. I played ball. Pitched. Years after I was married!

Pranks and general devilment stand out in the memories of several people, when they think back to their youth. It was all a part of growing up in the valley.

◆

Ernie Hanna: When the pigs were real little, us kids fed them. We always milked a bunch of cows, and we'd mix up a barrel or two of ground feed and throw the slop water in it and the milk in it to feed them when they were little. But I mean, it wasn't long until they were big enough to go on their own. Three or four of my cousins used to come up. Their uncle had been a minister in Williston. And they'd spend their summers with us. And that one, second oldest, I guess—well, they were the wildest bunch anyway. When they would see those old sows—I mean, they were laying all over with ten or twelve pigs—and someone said, "I betcha don't dare suck that old sow." She grabbed the little pig away and gets right down there. They'd do anything!

◆

Gerald Loring Boyer: When I think back on all the crazy things we did as kids, I shake my head, but some of those were so funny I still laugh with reckless abandon when I remember them. Probably, one of the funniest was tossing a half-wild tomcat with very large claws onto a pile of sleeping pigs. They would squeal, snort, roar, and nearly blast the walls down as they charged out of the pig pen. No one knows how the tomcat survived to wander back to the farm. Steer riding was a great sport as you would fill the mangers with bales and walk along the rails until you found a likely mount. With a mighty leap you jumped on his back and away you went until you were tossed in the manure. Strange how that was so much fun. (excerpt from *Memories*)

✦

Ernie Hanna: We had a steel hand-pump. And well, the second younger sister to me, she went and stuck her tongue on it once. It was about forty below, I guess, and they had to go in and get hot water and cloths, and blow on it, to get her tongue from it. Even so, I think it took all the hide off it.

✦

Margaret Pick: I wasn't old enough, but the neighbour's kids were the same age as Karen and me and in our class. They had four girls. So they got out Halloweening. Went to this Nat Morrison who lived right by the Monson School. Halfway to Goodwater. And oh, they saddled the cattle or harnessed them, and all this kind of stuff, you know. But when they went to go home, their horses were gone.

Gerald Pick: Old Nat took all the horses and tied them up in his barn.

Margaret Pick: So of course then they had to go the next day and ask for their horses back, you know.

Gerald Pick: This neighbour lived just half a mile down the road from us. And he went to the barn, and here his horses were all tied where his cows belonged and his cows were all tied up and harnessed. And he figured we did it. Well, I didn't. But he just kind of grinned. Then about a week afterwards, we come down to his place. "You know," he said, "I accused you boys of going up there. And," he says, "I found out this morning that it wasn't you, for sure. So I thought I'd come and tell you." "Well, how did you find out for sure?" Well, he says, "You know," he said—he had some black chickens, about a dozen of them, and that morning he went in to feed them, and he just kind of looked around his coop. No black chickens in it any more. So then he says, "I got to wondering where my black chickens was." And his brother-in-law was there, and said, "Well, you know, the other kid butchered all his own chickens, and now he's got a whole bunch of black ones." "So now," he says, "I know who did my barn, and where my black chickens are."

Margaret Pick: Stupid things. Our sons went on out on Halloween and came back with some chickens. And they picked them. And they were going to have chicken. The old hens were so tough, they never did get to cook them.

✦

Margaret Pick: Anyway, I had a school teacher. Gerry and a friend, they went down there where he lived, and they pushed this old cream separator and this old threshing machine down over the river. And they saddled all the cattle, and I guess they done everything they could. They swiped a bunch of chickens from him and brought them back and put them in Henry's chicken coop. For Halloween. Henry went out the next day and there's these terrible old chickens in there. He says, "If you're going to steal something, you could have at least stolen some decent chickens." Oh, he done everything!

◆

Ruby Gardipie Gauthier: Grandma had a dreadful little dog called Fanny. She was a scrawny little thing and very old. One day when Grandma and Grandpa had gone to Estevan, Fanny succumbed to an accidental blow to her head by a blunt instrument. This, of course, necessitated a funeral and it was a grand affair. Evelyn pulled the dearly departed in one of the little wagons followed by Aunt Aggie, who I believe was the priest. It sticks in my mind that Aunt Mickey was the undertaker. Uncle George was singing snatches from the mass in Latin. Vince, Pearl, and I were the mourners and this splendid procession was topped off by Uncle Frankie who was sawing away on Grandpa Boyer's violin, supplying the musical touch. Old Fanny went out in style. (excerpt from *Memories*)

. . . Monson's Grove

Adults played, too. Monson's Grove was perhaps the most popular place for picnics, dances, ball games, and general good times.

◆

Uncle Ernie Hanna: Monson's Grove. A road went back in there. It's all growed up to trees and brush and weeds now. Then, it was all open—if you went in a ways—next to the hill where the big round spot of old prairie was. They had a ballground and baseball. They'd go down around Sundays. And they used to have dances there. They'd built a dance pavilion there and they had that in there for quite a few years, too. People come from all over.

◆

Ernie Hanna: Yeah, that was just a mile and a half up from the ranch, you know. Up to the Monson's Grove. Well, sometimes there was a ball game and whatnot up there, and a rodeo down at the ranch at the same time. But if there was nothing doing down at the ranch, well, I mean, you'd be up there every Sunday for a picnic. Well, when my wife worked there, they sold soft drinks and hamburgers and hot dogs and stuff like that. And everybody gathered there every Sunday to play ball and stuff. So there'd be quite a crowd around there every Sunday. And they had dances every Saturday night there.

Monson's Grove was a popular site for community gatherings—picnics, dances, ball games. Here valley residents participate in a softball tournament in 1934. Another form of "entertainment" indulged in at Monson's Grove was to race cars up the side of the valley to see who could get the farthest. *Courtesy Roy McKague, Tribune*

Carl Hauglum: Oh, a beautiful place. Nice big dance hall down there. And lots of trees all where the building was and all along the grounds. A real picnic grounds. Seats all over.

Margaret Hauglum: Really nice. It was nice and level, where they had the picnic and the ball game. It was all up against the river. And then there was a hill on the other side where the men who thought they had the best cars would—

Carl Hauglum: —try to go up the steep hill. Yeah, real steep. Some of them didn't make it. One or two guys that made it, the way they did it was to go halfways up and then spin out.

✦

Wayne Pick: Play ball in the summer.

Margaret Pick: Softball. Just whoever was there.

Gerald Pick: Bunch of neighbours get together.

Margaret Pick: We played all over, but

Monson's Grove was the place where there was regular ball games. They called themselves the River Rats. And they were grown men. And they used to play. And of course other teams from Weyburn, Estevan, all over—you know they had some real ball tournaments. This went every Sunday, there was ball games.

◆

Carl Hauglum: Quite a few ball teams used to be on the river. The River Rats. You heard of them? They had a good ball team. All lived on the river there. Damn right, they were one of the better teams.

... good-time places

But any farmer's field could also serve as a baseball diamond, and there were other places in the valley where people gathered for a good time.

◆

Helen Blondeau: In the summertime, we used to have a ball diamond down where I lived, and they'd come playing ball every Sunday. Yeah, there was a ball diamond right on our land. I don't know—I guess there was a patch that they didn't put in wheat that was closer to the hill, and it was kind of too gumboed. And they made a baseball diamond down there, and they used to come and play every Sunday down there. And then they'd make a picnic and bring their lunches and have picnics.

◆

Carl Hauglum: And most farmers had a ball team in their pasture. Most of them had cattle—a lot of pasture. Now there's no land left—it's all broke up.

◆

Arnold Molstad: I think people were happier then than they are now. At least you knew your neighbours. You know when we see our neighbours now? It's in town. We don't visit one another.

Ball games. Any place there was prairie. I had a field I broke up here on section 13. That thing was more tramped down by ball players than by cattle.

◆

Marceline Lajimodiere: Yeah, we used to have picnics. In May sometimes—that was the long weekend. We used to go and have it at MacDonald Lake. They used to come there—all that bunch from west had a picnic there.

◆

Margaret Hauglum: We always had picnics in the summer. Like communities would have a picnic at the school, you know.

◆

Bella Gardipie: We had picnics in the summertime. Everybody'd all get together and go out to Lake MacDonald. We even used to make homemade ice cream. I don't know how they ever did it. But it was good. We'd make it after we got down there. I guess they used to bring the ice. Everybody around used to go.

✦

Clara Ziehl: In summer, we had a picnic, like a Sunday School picnic. And there were closing-of-school picnics. They were really something, you know. Everybody came and you got so dressed up.

✦

Helen Blondeau: Well, we'd eat potato salads and then they'd bring sandwiches and fresh onions from the garden. Lettuce. I don't remember them eating so much wieners and stuff like they do now. They'd make some kind of meat sandwiches.

. . . dances and parties

Dances and parties, either in people's homes or in the schoolhouses, were usually on the go. This was especially true in the wintertime when there was less work to do on the farm or ranch, and when the good cheer of neighbours was particularly important to break up the long, cold season.

✦

Uncle Ernie Hanna: Yeah. And then they had house parties, and there used to be a whole lot of dancing at the parties in the schoolhouses. That's when they come from all over. Yeah. They don't have any of that going on any more, I don't think.

✦

Ernie Boyer: Yeah, they had quite a few dances, and card parties. There was quite a bit going on. Pretty near every week. Somebody would have a birthday or something.

✦

Edgar Sawyer: Well, there was more community life at that time than there is today, you know. They had their house parties in the wintertime—not so much in the summer, but when the work was pretty well over, like harvest. Then they would have house parties, dances, and card parties. Oh yes.

Dancing and music were important parts of life. This harmonica part, found at the Sawvell homestead (NE 1/4 18-5-12 W2), likely made a lively contribution to family entertainment. A good number of people played some sort of musical instrument and anyone who could square dance, waltz, two-step, polka, or even jig was welcome to join in. *Courtesy Western Heritage Services, Saskatoon*

✦

Hazel Molstad: We used to have school dances.

Arnold Molstad: Sure, your entertainment was in schoolhouses and stuff like that. Anybody who could swing a fiddle would play. And it was good music. Well, different generations take it different, eh?

Hazel Molstad: We liked more violin. Kids nowadays, they don't like a violin. They want a guitar.

Arnold Molstad: And there was a few accordion players. Fox trots, waltzes.

Hazel Molstad: Square dances, waltzes. Probably the same as they do now. They had the polka, too.

Arnold Molstad: And it used to wear you out!

Hazel Molstad: And there was a few that could jig. Everybody associated. We had dances at Laroque's place. I remember.

Arnold Molstad: Sure. Wherever there was room enough. You didn't have a big hall.

Hazel Molstad: There was house parties a lot, too. Homes didn't have floor covers on. You just had your wood, you know. I suppose if somebody started dancing on the floor here, it wouldn't last long.

Arnold Molstad: Our old floor was pretty well wore.

Hazel Molstad: We had to put in new flooring!

✦

Rose Boyer: Louis and my brother Arthur both played the fiddle and they would get someone with an accordion to have a house dance. They would send me to visit Aunt Agnes and when I returned, the linoleum would be rolled up. I knew that they were planning a dance in the house. People got together a lot in those days. The Cooleys had a bunch of boys and we had girls, so we had a ready made dance. (excerpt from *Memories*)

✦

An episode that is close to Etta McDonald's heart is the story of wild geese that became pets. These geese seemed to be very fond of music and every time the geese heard the music from McDonald's organ, they would march right into the house and sit in a circle around the organ for all the world like a choir and quietly listen to the music. When the music stopped they quietly filed out and went back to the river. (excerpt from *Recollections of the Past*)

✦

Uncle Ernie Hanna: They had parties in schoolhouses, the people did in them days. And they'd have their parties in their house. Dancing. One thing and another. Once in a while. Well, we used to have big parties.

✦

Margaret Pick: Oh, they had square dancing all my growing-up years. That was the thing, because it was so interesting.

Gerald Pick: Square dances and the polka.

Margaret Pick: Schottische. The two-step.

The Ziehl family was one of the first to settle in the area of Monson's Grove. Here, family and friends gather at the dance pavilion located at the grove to celebrate the Ziehl's fiftieth wedding anniversary. *Courtesy Kathleen Hancock, Midale*

But we all loved that square dancing the best. You know, you'd get one man in the group that didn't know how to do it, and you'd get a hold of him and pull him around. Like my husband.

✦

Elizabeth Boyer Tisdale: My older brother Wilfred used to take me with him to dances in Hitchcock and Macoun. He was a great brother. After he left and got married Francis was the one that took us girls around. We used to have a lot of fun during the war and there was always a dance to go to every week. Frankie used to serenade me about my current boyfriend all the way to the dance and all the way home. I never could get mad at him. He used to get such a bang out of teasing me. (excerpt from *Memories*)

✦

Carl Hauglum: Oh, house parties.
Margaret Hauglum: Visited back and forth to the neighbours.

Carl Hauglum: Yeah, they don't do that no more. All the neighbours—three or four neighbours come together and got to one place for card playing. House dances.

Margaret Hauglum: Oh yeah, anybody that had a good-sized living room—nobody could afford carpets—a lot of them didn't even have linoleum. They had a bare floor. Put wax on there and dance.

Carl Hauglum: Couldn't hurt anything.

Margaret Hauglum: Oh yeah. Accordion.

Carl Hauglum: She plays the piano a lot. She played for a lot of dances. She quit playing the piano when the kids were going to school. She'd come home at three or four o'clock in the morning and have to get the kids off to school, so she said, "Enough of that!" Well, the dance was thirty or forty miles away sometimes. Play for a dance and come home late in the morning. Tired out all the next day. Didn't get much anyways— two or three dollars?

Margaret Hauglum: Well, you got more than that, maybe ten dollars a night or something like that.

Carl Hauglum: For the group?

Margaret Hauglum: No, ten dollars apiece. That was pretty good pay, we figured.

✦

Marceline Lajimodiere: Oh, there was house dances. We had good times. Better times than what the kids have now. We had dances and pretty near every third boy played the violin. And calling square dances and everything. Waltzes and everything. We had real good times, real fun time to go dancing.

✦

Ernie Hanna: The four of them in the band used to play the violin and the ukulele. One played piano. They used to have a really good orchestra. Two were playing the violin—one would be playing one guy's violin and be fingering the other's, you know.

✦

Margaret Pick: And then dances, Saturday night. Oh, we still had dances after I was fairly grown up. You'd go outside, if you drank and had a drink, and back in and dance.

Gerald Pick: But I don't think there was much drinking, at that time. There wouldn't be one bottle of liquor to where there are ten now. If you had a drink at a dance, well one, and that was it.

Margaret Pick: Everybody would go to the dance, and everybody danced with everybody. Not like it is nowadays. Now you go with a partner and that's who you dance with. Back then everybody danced with everybody.

✦

Jack Muirhead: We used to have parties.

Joyce Muirhead: Yeah, I've got some great party pictures. Every time we had a chance—like it was somebody's birthday: "Oh, we're going to have a party." All the neighbours did that.

And we would all go. All the people in the valley would go.

Jack Muirhead: Well, we had other people, too, going to the parties.

Joyce Muirhead: People from on the top, yes.

Jack Muirhead: Friends.

Joyce Muirhead: But our valley friends were our good friends.

✦

Edgar Sawyer: Well, I don't think that anybody ever suffered here, you know. In the thirties, they shipped carloads of potatoes and carloads of codfish and apples and all that stuff from the east, you know. Cheese. Yeah, and beans.

I can remember what we done for entertainment. I went to a dance one night at these people's place, and this is what they give us for lunch at midnight. She had baked beans in one of them big old bean kettles. You know, with the handles on them? And she brought that out, and just come along with a plate and you had beans.

✦

Clara Ziehl: Once in a while in the wintertime, we used to get in the sleigh, a whole bunch of us. We used to go to the neighbours', you know. And the old folks played cards, while us kids tore the house down.

The Hanna Ranch, shown here in 1930, periodically hosted rodeos where cowboys competed for top honours. After the activities, neighbours and acquaintances had a chance to visit and take part in the evening dance that followed. *Courtesy Clara Ziehl, Midale*

The Hanna Ranch as it was in 1930. In addition to rodeos, friends and neighbours also gathered here for other social and work-related occasions. The busiest times of the year were spring and fall round-ups. *Courtesy Clara Ziehl, Midale*

. . . the Hanna Ranch rodeo

Rodeos were a natural part of the valley entertainment—just about everyone had horses and knew how to ride them. The Hanna Ranch was famous for its rodeo.

✦

Ernie Hanna: Well, we used to have a crowd lots of times on Sundays. You'd get a crowd like that and we used to have a small rodeo, you might say, every Sunday.

✦

Margaret Pick: We used to have some real good stampedes down there. Even riders from Alberta.

✦

Ernie Hanna: Yeah, Sundays. I mean, even after Mom was gone. Sometimes the wife, she'd cook for maybe forty or fifty that come in and have supper after the rodeo—or the challenge of who could ride the best. And we had an old buckaroo mare—we called her Roan. She got so—I mean, you know, you could just about walk up and throw the saddle on her, and that little crowd, they all holler, "I'll ride her, I'll ride her!" They turn her out the gate and

This is the Hanna Ranch site in 1988. All that marks the spot now are a cellar (the small collection of stones seen slightly to right of centre on the near side of the fence) and the old well. The trees seen here were planted by the Hanna family. *Courtesy Western Heritage Services, Saskatoon*

hardly any of them could ride her.

✦

Ernie Hanna: Well, we started out with purebred Oregon running-stock and crossed them with a Clyde, and those horses were known certainly all over the United States for rodeo horses. Some of the guys would come down to the rodeo and they seen that oarlock brand on them, and they said, "Christ, take me home!"

✦

Uncle Ernie Hanna: Rodeos? Well, you had to set on one of them wild ones—if you were going to make any money. You had to be setting on there pretty good to get any money. Because there's a lot of good riders, too. But I was lucky enough to take first money. I got a few bucks. Maybe 160 bucks.

✦

Gerald Pick: You know, when you talk to these kids, it can kind of get embarrassing sometimes. My older son—we were talking about old Ernie Hanna and his oldest son. And I just said to Kirk, "You know, old Ernie would get on things that Tommy could scarce to walk up to." Be damned if Kirk didn't ask Tommy about that in front of me, one time. Well, Tommy got out of it pretty good. He just laughed: "Well," he said, "I'll tell you. Your dad could be right, because when the old man rode horses, you snubbed up to a post to get on top and you turned them loose yourself. And while you're bending over un-loosening that halter rope, you had to watch that they didn't jump out from under you right then! When I rode, they rigged a chute and I was setting on him before they turned him out. I still don't brag that I can ride as good as Ernie did. He did it alone, where there's four men helping you now."

✦

Ernie Hanna: Yeah. One rodeo, Ernie got so drunk I guess that he couldn't even hardly walk. And somebody bet him—I don't know—five or ten dollars that he couldn't ride a bare-back. He says, "Hell, I can ride him without any-thing." And he just took one hand on the mane and one hand on the tail, and he rode it. Yeah, he used to take first money out around Ponteix and Aneroid and all through that country. And he had—I forget what he called him now—Whitesocks, I guess it was. Yeah, that's right. A bay Clyde. He used to have a white face and four white feet. He'd ride him as much as eighty miles to a rodeo, and pull the saddle off and throw him in the corral. And, by God, nobody could ride him. He'd get on him

after the rodeo and rode him home again.

✦

Margaret Pick: And I can remember what we done was make ice cream with ice, and turning the ice-cream maker. And then Mom sold it to the people at the rodeo. Ice cream cones. We had three or four ice-cream makers and that's what we done, turning the ice cream.

✦

Ernie Hanna: I don't know. In about 1928, '29, '30, or something—I forget what year it was—we had a bear at the rodeo. And we had this one granary we showed there: we had dug out a bunch of wild coyotes. Had coyotes in there. You know, anybody could come along and see the coyotes in the granary there. And then we had—Dad traded for it—this bear. And we had a post right out in here, and that bear—Dad got him so he'd crawl up that post, you know. And he was kind of a skinny sort of a bear. You know, a black bear. Not very big. The way he'd whine and cry—but then if Dad got after him, why up the pole he'd go.

✦

Margaret Pick: I can remember. He got a bear from someplace. And he had that thing on a chain and it used to walk around and around and around. And we even had that in the rodeo. My young sister, she charged for people to come and watch this bear.

Ernie Hanna: And, oh golly, I don't remember what all animals we had in there. Seems to me we had some badgers there, too. And they were hard to keep, because you had to have a wire floor as well as wire sides. They'd dig out otherwise. And coyotes, and some wild ducks, you know. We had little fences. We had all kinds of animals lined along there where everybody could go and look at them. Well, we had sheep and everything like that. But I can remember having them coyotes in there, and that bear!

...going to town

Another form of entertainment was the trip to town. The trip itself was usually made for practical reasons, such as buying supplies or taking the grain to the elevator, but these trips offered a change of pace for the valley people. Especially for children and women, who didn't travel to town as often as the menfolk, going to town was a special treat.

Carl Hauglum: They had to go to Halbrite in the early days. And Macoun. But Midale didn't have a depot—just a siding and a boxcar. And shortly after they put a siding in there, they added a loading platform. Made of dirt, them days. Yeah, a lot of them did load in Halbrite and drove back to the valley. Halbrite was a big town in those days.

Three banks and three hotels. It was a little good-sized town.

Jack Boyer: Macoun? I suppose 180 people, maybe. It hasn't really grown. Maybe there's more than that there now. Now, you see, we can live in a small town and drive forty or fifty miles away and it don't mean nothing. But in those times, why people owned a horse and buggy or a Model-T Ford, and it takes a little while to travel. Because Weyburn was a long ways away from us at that time.

Helen Blondeau: Well, Macoun was quite a size at one time, too. It went right down. Because there was two or three stores there. There was two grocery stores, for sure, and two hardware stores. And a big hotel—burned down.

✦

John Dowhanuik: In them days we never got a chance to go to town. You could go to Outram, but there was nothing there. And Macoun was ten miles away. And we couldn't get across—because we lived on the south side of the river—and when the river was high, you couldn't make it. You had to go way around by Louis Boyer's. They finally built a bridge down there. So that was a long ways around there. Took about all day to get around to Macoun and back. So once a year—that was about all we went to town.

The prices in this 1936 advertisement for the general store in Macoun are enough to make anyone long for the "good old days." *Courtesy Arnold and Hazel Molstad, Outram*

◆

Edgar Sawyer: Yeah, the stores kept pretty well what you'd get today, you know. Pretty much the same. You didn't have it parcelled up like you do now, you know. They come in boxes of stuff. Prunes and dried apples and dried stuff. Come in these big boxes and you just took what you wanted. Cheese come in them big round wheels—sitting on the counter there, you know, and they'd cut you off a wedge.

◆

Ernie Boyer: Well, we never bought less than twenty pounds of sugar in a bag, and flour was in one-hundred-pound bags. There was fifty-pound bags for smaller families, but we never bought fifty pounds, we bought one hundred! And tea and coffee—you could buy by five or ten pounds. And it was bulk in beans, and you brought it home and you had a grinder and whenever you wanted some coffee you threw in a handful, ground it, and threw it in the pot. It was fresh, real fresh coffee. A lot of farmers would stock up for the winter, so they wouldn't have to go maybe until spring. Then by spring a lot of them would go to the store and charge for goods. They'd start charging in May and June. Well, the store people would carry them over till harvest time.

◆

Helen Blondeau: Well, we probably

canned our own fruit. Or bought dried fruit. They used to sell a lot of dried fruit years ago. Prunes and peaches and apples. And it came in big boxes, flat boxes. And I remember we used to buy a lot of that stuff.

◆

Edgar Sawyer: In Macoun we had two town halls, we had two livery barns, we had two garages, and we had two blacksmith shops. Three stores, a butcher shop, drugstore, hardware, lumberyard. We'd buy salt and sugar and matches and stuff like that, you know. Dad smoked and he had to get his tobacco. Old Chum, I think. And Union Leader, Old Chum and Union Leader. Because we had those little baskets, and we had them for dinner pails when we started school. So if he run out of matches or tobacco, why you went to town in a hurry!

◆

Arnold Molstad: Well, you'd buy some porridge and stuff like that. A lot of times, most of the time, you'd take your wheat to mill in Estevan. And you'd get some breakfast food and flour and everything right there. And you'd have it all. All it would cost you was the grinding.

◆

Helen Blondeau: Well, we'd up to town about once a week, I guess. We were about ten miles from Macoun. And we'd go to town and did what we wanted, I guess. Buy sugar, maybe, and jam and honey and porridge, oatmeal, flour. Well, sometimes you brought your wheat to town and they'd grind the flour, and we'd get the flour and all the bran, you know, in big bags and feed it to the pigs. Yeah, because they had a flour mill in Estevan at one time.

◆

Marceline Lajimodiere: Yeah, flour. When they had the flour mill here in Estevan, you used to bring your wheat there and get your flour. They made your flour—big sacks of flour.

◆

Edgar Sawyer: You wouldn't go to town any more than you had to. If you were milking cows and like that—shipping cream—why, you had to go to town to get your can, and go and take your other cream in. And then your eggs and stuff, you know. You didn't leave them sit around too long. You got rid of them, too. But in the winter, there'd be maybe two weeks at a stretch without going to town.

◆

Ernie Hanna: I remember the first winter we were married, I made quite a few trips to Estevan, hauling coal from Estevan with four horses on a sleigh. That's where we made a living. You know, you go down there and you get a load of coal for two or three dollars, bring it back up, and sell it for ten or

twelve. But we'd go down early in the morning. Clarence Huff and I travelled together a lot of times. And we'd make it to the old CPR pump house, and we'd stop and feed the horses and eat in the shade of that old pump house—out of the wind. And go on to Estevan and get loaded up and pull back into the livery stable and put the horses in the barn. And we'd sleep in one stall. The next morning we'd take off early and make it up that far to the pump house again, and have lunch and feed the horses.

◆

Margaret Hauglum: They slept with the horses in the barn in Estevan.
Carl Hauglum: Yeah, tied the horses up.
Margaret Hauglum: Usually in the manger, wasn't it?
Carl Hauglum: I slept there. That was the hotel—winter, when it got cold. But we slept outside a few times in nice weather. You could put a blanket down and lay on the ground. Tied the horses up. Took your dinner pail with you— you didn't buy your meals, even. You didn't have money. Broke in the thirties, you know. You were lucky to get fifty cents a day, if you could get a job. Dollar was a big wage.
Margaret Hauglum: Well, that's the reason why we picked the cow chips, because sometimes we didn't have the money to buy coal, eh?

◆

Clara Ziehl: Well, probably Mom went to town once a week if she got around to it, but I don't suppose us kids ever went hardly at all. I can remember how Mom used to always bring home a bag of candy. That had to do us for a week.

✦

Gerald Pick: Well, Halbrite kind of started going backward then. The municipal office was built in Midale. And that big hotel. And then they got the beer parlour there.

Margaret Pick: He was the first one that had a glass of beer in that beer parlour. He was only seventeen years old.

Wayne Pick: That's because Grandpa Pick owned it.

Gerald Pick: No, no, Vince Deacon owned it then. But we was hauling ice. The day he opened the bar—I think the only reason he let me in there—we was packing ice, my brother and I, for him. And we unloaded our ice and he said, "The beer parlour is officially opened." So in we went.

Margaret Pick: He drank for quite a little while before they decided he wasn't twenty-one.

Gerald Pick: Well, he was good though. Yeah. He didn't kick me out of that bar any time I went in there. But he met me out on the street and asked me not to come in there. But it wasn't him—it was the people. They wanted to close that bar down. And I could see his part, even at seventeen years old.

Well, then my dad and my uncle and I were working, once. And Dad and Uncle, they just decided that they should go in and have a beer. So I was going to stay home. "Oh, come on, come on." "Well, all right." I went into Midale. I knew I had other things I could do. But I was supposed to come in and have a beer with them and I said, "No." I said, "Old Vince asked me to stay out. I'm going to stay out." "Oh," Uncle Abe said, "I'll talk to Vince in there." So he got him in there all right and started talking to him. "Sure," Vince said, "Gerry can drink." He went in and got some beer and headed for his front room in the back of the hotel. They were bound I was going to drink beer with them.

✦

Gerald Pick: You know when you talk about kids doing things with cars and that. We were just as big a damn fools, you know, really, when I think of it. A street full of people—you know, a sidewalk—and we'd ride these goddamned saddle horses on the sidewalk, just for something to do. There was lots of other places to ride them, but we rode them down there. But the town cop, he'd just say, "Come on, you fellows. Get out there." And there was no putting you in jail or nothing else.

Margaret Pick: My dad got an old Model-T—his first car. And I don't know how he ever got to Midale with it, but he did. And my dad was quite a guy. And we always—I don't know why they couldn't have done something different—but we always had to stop and open the gate there at the ranch, pushing it. And he didn't pull the brake. My brother and his wife were down there with him. He was hollering "Whoa!" and went right through the gate with that car.

. . . a special place

For the children, especially, the valley was a playground.

✦

Jack Muirhead: The kids from Macoun used to think that was the greatest place—down in the valley there. Because I guess it was a novelty for them to come down and visit with us. They used to play the funniest games. Well, it is wild too there.

Joyce Muirhead: I'll tell you what they really enjoyed was all the adventure they could find. Like there was some caves over in the pasture below the house, and the kids had those made into playhouses, you know. And they'd make mud pies and all this stuff. Well, those kids in Macoun—their mothers wouldn't let them get their hands dirty. And I let them make mud pies and they made bread, and they made everything. And they had a flat stone and they used to put it out there in the sun to cook. They'd spend hours up there. And they'd get sticks or boards and make a table and make little stools for chairs. And the kids would come for the weekend and they'd just have a great time. I can remember, one little girl never wanted to go home. She wanted to stay. She said, "I just love making a mess." And here she was with her hands all muddy—making loaves of bread with mud. And she was having a ball.

Jack Muirhead: Yeah, the valley's a different world, really.

Joyce Muirhead: All the trees, and there was berries there. Saskatoons. And then the kids would go up in the hills and they'd explore up there. They had one great big rock we called an elephant rock. It's still there, just above the house where we were. And I don't know—those kids and my own kids spent half their lives on elephant rock. This was a castle, you know. And they could use their imagination so well. And then in the wintertime the kids all came for tobogganing on those hills, you know. And they had a great time. And if the river was half-decent, and not any snow, they would sweep a place off, and they spent hours down there skating. Well, you know—kids—that's the life, eh? They loved that. And they could go and do all those things without bothering anybody.

Hard Times in the Valley

There is a temptation in any collection of memories to include only those recollections that hark back to "the good old days." But that would not present a truthful picture of life in the valley. The hardships of the early settlers and the hard work of farming and ranching have already been recounted in these pages. However, there are other "hard" memories as well, and they deserve to be recorded.

... making ends meet

Part of the story of the valley is certainly the struggle to make ends meet, which everyone in the valley faced.

◆

Carl Hauglum: Well, I tell you, in the valley they thought they were a lower class of people down there. Well, they had nothing there. You were hard up as hell, you know. You had no land, living on the river bottom. Trapping is what they made their living on, most of them, I think. Worked outside the valley, if they had a job. And some of them had big families: eight, ten, twelve kids, you know. Poor folks, keeping that up. Of course they had their own cattle and milk and stuff, you know. Lived on that. Awfully hard.

Margaret Hauglum: People lived frugally in those days.

Carl Hauglum: Lived cheap.

Margaret Hauglum: Not like now.

Carl Hauglum: Lived cheap, yeah.

◆

Marceline Lajimodiere: My husband had a sister in town. We used to stop in and bring them something sometimes from the farm. Even during what they call the dirty thirties, we used to always grow enough vegetables. That time we had lots of water all over. The sloughs didn't go dry. The rivers didn't go dry. Nothing. And we always growed enough stuff. Feed for our pigs and chickens. And there was no grass to cut nowhere. But the thistles, they were like two or three feet high! Well, that's what the horses got to eat. Russian thistles. Green, they're soft, they're tender. Stock all ate that. They liked it and they milked good.

◆

Jack Muirhead: Sometimes the river was bone dry. We were planting potatoes in the river, and barley one year. Never cultivated or anything.

And the potatoes grew, and so did the barley. The barley—that was '31. The driest year we had, I suppose. And when that hailstorm come along—we'd just cut the barley a few days before and had it stacked—and this big hailstorm came along. Blew down the bridge. Well, it broke all the windows in our house. Somebody said about our old barn, "Why didn't it blow it away?" I think my brother said, "Well, there was too many places for the wind to blow through." So that's one reason the barn didn't blow away.

That was a sorry time. And I think it was the same year, we had a steer calf. We were going to save it for meat, and the doggone thing got hung up in the fence and died. And our crop froze that year. Boy! Oh, we had an awful year. But the saving of that year was the government was buying up hay, standing hay, and baling it and storing it. They paid us so much a ton for standing hay. I had no sale for hay that year, so I just sold the standing hay, and we had a pretty good bunch of hay. And so between that and selling the eggs and milking the cows, we survived.

I guess you might say we existed. You know, it was no big thing. Everybody has got the idea that anybody that lives along the river, they got it made. Everything is beautiful. Well, it's what you prefer, I suppose. But we done well. We were doing okay. I guess we didn't make a lot of money, but we were progressing real good, because we were building up a herd, and rais-

ing a family. And we had to move our whole operation from one side of the river to the other, and this is after the war, now, when we come back. But I guess I should go back to the time when we as a family were there. And then in the thirties was the dry years. And of course what can you do in the dry years? We couldn't even grow the feed.

✦

Ernie Hanna: Thirty-seven was the year that we had such a good crop down there. That was a year or two after Dad had passed away, when they took a crop report. They figured it would make fifty bushels to the acre. And it didn't make bran! It was rust. They had ten rows of heads on the wheat. And I of course was the last one to get any relief seed or anything like that. And so we didn't get no rust-resistant wheat or anything like that, you know. Yeah, it was just a lovely crop, but I mean, it just rusted until there wasn't a thing in it.

✦

Marceline Lajimodiere: That's why I say, we don't think of those things, you know. Now, when I come to think, I never paid attention when the people talked about things. Like my dad and two other men—they used to haul freight from Winnipeg to Regina. And there was no railroad. It's a long ways. People can't believe those things. We don't talk about those things, because the younger generation don't believe it. People worked for fifty cents a day. Young people ask you, "Well, why'd you do that for? You were crazy to do that." You have to have money—some money. No matter if you didn't have to buy your meat and different things like that. You still have to have money to buy your other supplies, like sugar and tea and so.

I'm glad I never owned any land—farm land. And my husband was raised on the farm and everything, and just living like that. Never get ahead. And I said, "I can't be this way." Never have anything. Always skimping from one year to another. My husband thought if we'd leave the farm, he'd starve to death. "Well," he said, "I don't know anything else." "Well," I said, "you'll learn. All the years you work at a job, you get paid. On the farm, you work your head off—and no money."

... death

Death is also a part of the valley story. Especially in the early days, death was an immediate part of life—there were no fancy funeral homes in the valley, no undertakers who would look after things. As in every other aspect of valley life, people looked after themselves, and death—whether from natural causes or from accidents—was another fact that had to be confronted.

✦

Jack Boyer: We had a neighbour. I remember I was quite young at the time. I remember he was a rancher and he was kind of sick. I don't know what he had, but he used to come over to our place. And I remember a lot of times, he'd come in up here, and he'd go in and lay down and rest for a while. The poor old guy finally died. I suppose he had cancer and didn't know what he had. I don't know—I wouldn't say cancer, but he was sick. He was quite old. I suppose he was in his sixties or seventies. But I remember him so well. He used to come over to our place quite often. Kind of nice old fellow. I was just a small kid at the time.

✦

Rose Boyer: Someone came and told Grandpa that his pigs were out and were in someone's field. So Grandpa and Grandma Boyer went to chase the pigs home. Grandpa chased them until he couldn't go any farther and then he took the buggy so Grandma could help chase them. After a while she noticed the horses running loose and saw him fall off the wagon. He was dead. (excerpt from *Memories*)

✦

Arnold Molstad: Well, this Mr. Klyne, he got killed by the train. Walking on the tracks.

Hazel Molstad: He was deaf, you see, and he couldn't hear it. But he'd do that many times, and he usually stepped off. But this time he didn't, and the train couldn't stop in time.

The great wars also took their toll on the Prairies. Sons and husbands left to serve their country and never returned. The above photograph is of the Boyer and Blondeau families. *Courtesy Norman Blondeau, Macoun*

Jack Boyer: I remember the old fellow, but he was an old, old man at the time. And I can't remember when he died, but I remember how this fellow died. He was hit by a train. This one. He was deaf and he was walking on the darn railroad track—didn't hear the train coming.

✦

Carl Hauglum: My uncle lived at this one place for a while. And he had a baby that died, and they buried it right in the yard there. Well, they had no funeral to report in them days. The baby was just born, you know. Made a little box and buried it by the side of the buildings. I can remember where it was yet. But you can't find it now—all rotten. You know we used wood for the gravemarker.

✦

Margaret Pick: What I remember so distinctly was my older sister had a boy—and he was what they call a blue baby. And he didn't live too long. Mom stayed home with Clara and the rest of us went out, because we had parts in the Christmas play. When we came back, he was gone. I'll never forget that. Funny how things like that stay in your mind, you know.

✦

Hazel Molstad: There was one neighbour that had the son that drowned in the river.

Arnold Molstad: He lived right on the flat. His quarter's right there. His son drowned. Hailstorm come up from the valley—the river bed filled with water. And he was down at Laroque's. The boy's horse started to swim and just turned over. After that, the man, he sold out and went away.

✦

Ernie Boyer: Art Jones, A.R. Jones. His son drowned when he was fourteen years old in the river. And he was my chum. We used to always go together. They moved out about 1922, because his son drowned in 1921. He was fourteen years old. I used to go to school with him. He used to be my chum. He was going across with a horse. I don't know what happened. The horse must have hit him some way and hurt him.

. . . storms and floods

As sure as death (and taxes) was bad weather.

✦

Margaret Pick: Some neighbours built a little house just north of Doc's Park, and a cyclone come along and it demolished that house. There was him and his wife and their oldest son. And they were both out looking for the baby—it was sleeping in the crib—and he found the baby and he ran up the hill to what was Doc's Park there. And I guess she nearly went crazy trying to find him and the baby. And the baby wasn't harmed. None of them were. And they said they found pieces of their stuff over half a mile away from that house. Just absolutely demolished it.

◆

Jack Boyer: In '47 we had an awful lot of snow. Oh boy, was there ever. I re-

member, I went up to this Hobert's place one time in the winter, and the snow was piled up to the top of the telephone pole.

◆

Gerald Pick: You know you're talking about the Great Depression of the

It was not uncommon for the Souris River to flood its banks. It was a predicament the residents simply had to deal with—so they did. *Courtesy Jack and Joyce Muirhead, Estevan*

thirties, and I have argued that it has been drier this last few years in this country than it ever was in the thirties. Because in the thirties, well, all down in the flats and around there, there was stock running. And you was riding a saddle horse pretty near belly deep in snow. Well, that snow all melted and ran into the river. And you haven't had such a thing for the last six years. No snow around here at all. So right in this part of the country, it's a lot drier than it was then. The only thing we haven't had that they had in the thirties is wind.

Storms, deep snow, and drought are a part of the natural history of the entire prairie region, but the valley people had to contend with another of nature's forces as well—floods. Almost everyone in the valley has stories of flash floods, breaks in the dam, or just plain high water.

✦

Margaret Pick: I couldn't believe it. We went through the valley a few years ago, going up to the park up at Halbrite, and I couldn't believe that the river was so low. And of course when we got floods—we had a flood when we lived down there and we had to move out. We went up to my sister's. The river here, it came right through here. The whole flat was flooded. The house was up on the hill, and it was a good halfway up on the barns.

Gerald Pick: It just missed the house, but the barn was flooded with water.

Margaret Pick: Unless you see a flood like that you can't believe it. The water was just swirling right through everything. But there wasn't too much to wreck at our place.

Gerald Pick: Not too much to wreck. But when they talk about this dam [Rafferty-Alameda], it makes me mad. That water came up while we were living there—it happened about six times. But by July I was running a fence along the river to keep the livestock I had in the pasture, because that river was only about two feet deep, and they just walked across it.

Margaret Pick: Yeah, when it went low, we could walk across it.

✦

John Dowhanuik: The problem with having a barn on the flats was when the water got up high, the barn was always in the water. That's why we had to move it. In the years when my brother-in-law lived down there, there was no water. When we lived down there afterwards, the river backed up into our ravine, and we had water halfway to the house. The flat was all under water. So then we built a barn on the hill above.

✦

Edgar Sawyer: Oh gosh, I've seen it flood up to the Laroque's—the windows in the Laroque's house. Different times. But they could've just moved a little ways one way or the other, and been up on the dry land. But they wanted to be beside the water, I guess.

✦

John Dowhanuik: The Laroques had a barn right on the flats. Right on the flats there, and every time the water come, they had to anchor the barn down. Their house was on the flat, too. A three- or four-room house, you know. A two-storey house. Every time the flood come in, they had to move out. That two-storey house—you could just see the top of it, when the water went through. The water would come up twenty feet high—that house was over twenty feet and you could just see the top of it. They had the house anchored so the flood wouldn't take the house away. And all their buildings, too— they were all tied up.

✦

Jack Boyer: Yeah, well—1976. It flooded in the spring and then they had a heavy rain at Yellowgrass. After it rained at Yellowgrass Marsh—they had five inches of rain there—it flooded the whole valley again in June. It over- flowed the crop, you know. There was no need of that at all. Our house wasn't flooded. See where we lived, we were approximately fifteen feet above the river bank. And it just run, oh, I'd say about seven, eight feet, right in the valley. And you're under water for about ten days. Cross the road? You couldn't get across the valley! Oh yeah. We had a four-foot raised road there— four and a half foot, I think it was— and there was over a foot of water on that road. Ten days. Imagine the amount of water went through at that time. And now, they got nothing.

✦

Ernie Hanna: When the water was high in the river in the spring, you couldn't get across. Why, my sister Clara would stay at one neighbour's place and I stayed over at another neighbour's place. Well, every spring it used to flood. I mean the banks would be com- pletely full and part of that flat out there would be under water, you know.

Esther Hanna: I can remember one bad one we had. And we came down to where the Monson bridge is. Well, there was a bachelor that lived there. Floyd Pepperlin? He came up in a boat and he got us—my folks—my mother and I and I'm sure my dad was there, too. But I was only five years old, or less than that, I guess. The water was right to the house and all the way down the valley.

Ernie Hanna: Yeah, the valley was flooded there right on up past the Horsman's. But the water never did get in the house. Where the horse barn was, it used to get up right just about around to the foundation of the horse barn, but it never flooded where the cow barns were. But the sheds, way down—that would be flooded.

✦

Jack Muirhead: Remember that time Owen came home in the spring? He'd been into school.

This photo of the Souris River in flood was taken from the Gilles farm (NE 1/4 10-3-10 W2) around 1976 or 1978. *Courtesy Jack Boyer, Moose Jaw*

Joyce Muirhead: Yes, I'll never forget that.

Jack Muirhead: How did he get home? He walked across the bottom of the hill.

Joyce Muirhead: Carrying his shoes.

Jack Muirhead: And he had to cross the river, and the river was breaking up. And she went and got him and brought him across the river.

Joyce Muirhead: He got up to this other side, and there was water about a foot deep on the ice. And he had his shoes in his hand. He didn't want to get his shoes dirty. He was a fussy, wee boy. And I said, "Owen, just come across." And the water was running fast. And he was scared. And I was terrified. And Jack wasn't home. And I thought,

"Well, okay, he can't stay there, because the ice is going to come down any minute, and I've got to go and get him." And I went across—and my heart was in my mouth—and I picked him up and carried him. And that ice was breaking up as I walked. We made it to this side, but I don't know how. Somebody was holding my hand, because it shouldn't have been.

Jack Muirhead: Well, it wasn't deep, but still, to go into that icy water—

Joyce Muirhead: Oh, I'll never forget that. That's one thing that I'll live with forever was that poor little kid standing there with his shoes in his hand, and terrified to come over. And I was just as scared on the other side. But what are you going to do? You can't leave him over there. And the ice came down in half an hour. He'd perish over there. I had to go. I never was so terrified or scared. Did I ever pray so hard as I did that time?

✦

Margaret Pick: After we moved away from the valley, it was worse yet. That's when the flood took that railroad bridge out up by Monson's Grove. You've heard of that? Yeah, there was a bridge going across there for the railroad. And about fifty years ago, well, everything went down river.

Gerald Pick: A lot of people who built along the flats had their houses wrecked.

✦

Jack Muirhead: The year before that, the flood came down in the summer. Fifty-three I guess it was.

Joyce Muirhead: Oh gosh.

Jack Muirhead: The flood come down in the summer. They got twenty-one inches of rain in the Yellowgrass area. They got twenty-one inches of rain up there, and of course that's the headwaters of the Souris. And it just flooded this whole area. What you call a sum-

Western Heritage Services archaeologists crossing the ford at the Muirhead homestead (SW 1/4 34-2-9 W2). This is the spot Joyce Muirhead had to drive across during the summer flood. When the river is high, the road is entirely covered by water. *Courtesy Western Heritage Services, Saskatoon*

mer flood—'53. Flooded us out completely. And our son Owen was going to school, and we used to have to take the tractor across this flooded river and up the dyke and across the bottom of the hill, and then we'd take the truck and go from there to take him to school. Everything was flooded out. But I had to go and work. I'd got a job looking after the hay plot south of Midale there. Well, when I was away, Joyce had to take him across to school. But when she's going across a body of water in the tractor, she drifts.

Joyce Muirhead: I cannot do it.

Jack Muirhead: And we only had a stone crossing. So if you drift off that, you know what happens. I pounded posts in along as a guide for her on one side of the crossing. Be damned if she wasn't going over the other side!

Joyce Muirhead: I can't. When I get in the middle—

Jack Muirhead: —so I pounded the posts on both sides, so she had to go between. So she did.

Joyce Muirhead: I'm steering where I'm floating. I feel like the tractor's floating. I can't do it. I can't go across water.

Jack Muirhead: As far as she was concerned, the tractor was floating. It wasn't. She was going with the current.

Joyce Muirhead: Yeah, and it's a terrible thing.

Jack Muirhead: But you know, you're not supposed to look at the water. You're supposed to look ahead.

Joyce Muirhead: I wasn't. I tried to.

Jack Muirhead: I put posts on both sides

of the crossing so she couldn't make a mistake.

✦

Arnold Molstad: But that dam broke once. Yeah. And then the water went right up to the windows in the old CPR pump house there.

Hazel Molstad: That was just because that dam broke. That would never, never happen otherwise.

Arnold Molstad: Well, it was a wall of water came down. We had a granary down my side of the road where the steel bridge used to be. And it just wiped that right out.

Hazel Molstad: And it happened in the middle of the night. There was a family living there and this guy's brother.

Arnold Molstad: Well, Ernie Boyer's son there.

Hazel Molstad: And his brother saw this coming and he told her to get out. Well, they lost their chickens and pigs and a lot of that stuff. But I guess they got the family out.

Arnold Molstad: Sometimes at the Laroque's, the water would get in there so they'd have to move their stuff upstairs in the house.

Hazel Molstad: Then they'd go to the barn in a boat.

✦

Helen Blondeau: Those dykes didn't do any good, I don't think, to anything. They were supposed to keep the flood out, but I don't think it did. It flooded one year—'43—when the dam broke

Rising water from the Souris River covers the site of the abandoned CPR water pump station. The dyke, built to hold back the water, is almost invisible. Through the years, valley inhabitants suffered through a number of floods, and fires too. In 1914 a tragic hotel fire in Macoun took a number of lives, and one home, the telephone exchange, the barber shop, and the butcher shop were also destroyed. Other fires in the same town in 1911 and 1929 caused extensive damage as well. *Courtesy Norman Blondeau, Macoun*

at Midale dam. Then it flooded. The valley flooded. Yeah. We sure didn't like that flood, because our house got flooded—that pump house. The water came about a foot high on the floor. And of course it ruined all the floors. That was in '43.

◆

Jack Muirhead: You see, in the thirties, the late thirties, they came in and they built those dykes. And they built Midale dam, and there was a big scheme to irrigate—flood irrigate. And it never worked, because in 1943 the first time they ever got any water, that washed the dam out. Yeah, '43 was a big flood. They had a hell of a storm here in March. But they repaired the dam afterwards, and '48—another big year, another big flood—it washed the dam out again. Washed a hole in it, that is. So they repaired it again, and then they dug the spillway down, so the blamed thing doesn't hold any water any more. That dam was supposed to back the water up to where Mainprize Park is, I suppose. That would have all been flooded up in that area. Well, it's a big dyke, but you get any weight of water behind that and there's no way it's going to hold. You know, the design is not there. And I think that's true for any small dam.

◆

Edgar Sawyer: Oh well, them little dams—they didn't build much of

Little remains of the former Macoun Bridge, shown above. *Courtesy Western Heritage Services, Saskatoon*

anything at that time, you know. Yes of course it helped to hold the water, for those that needed it. But their structure wasn't made strong enough to take any amount of water. The water would go over the top and wash them out. The beavers could make a better one!

A contemporary photograph of the Souris River Valley. *Courtesy Souris Basin Development Authority*

Conclusion

These chapters have offered a brief glimpse into the history of the Souris Valley, and tell only a part of the story. There were many other people we could have interviewed for this book who would undoubtedly have been able to add much more to the oral history presented here; their memories are as important as any preserved in these pages.

This is certainly not the end of the process. The story of "them days" continues whenever people from the valley get together to reminisce, whenever old times are recalled. Those who remember the way life was in the valley are a living archive—a living history book—and they continue to educate us with their special knowledge. Their responsibility is a serious one.

As for the rest of us, we also have a responsibility—to listen. The experiences of the old-timers will soon fade if we do not hear their voices, and listen to their stories. It is a responsibility we all share, for by doing so we honour the early settlers, as well as their children, who carry this history in their memories.

This collection is a small tribute to these keepers of history. A greater tribute is a community's continued interest in its past, and its further efforts to collect and preserve the memories of "them days."

People Interviewed

Helen Blondeau interviewed by Michael Taft, 12 July 1990, Midale.

Norman Blondeau interviewed by Michael Taft, 25 July 1990, Macoun.

Ernie Boyer interviewed by Olga Klimko, 16 July 1988, Midale.

Jack Boyer interviewed by Michael Taft, 24 July 1990, Moose Jaw.

John Dowhanuik interviewed by Olga Klimko, 26 July 1988, Hitchcock.

Bella Gardipie interviewed by Olga Klimko, 15 July 1988, Estevan.

*Uncle Ernie Hanna interviewed by Olga Klimko, 18 July 1988, Midale.

Ernie and Esther Hanna interviewed by Michael Taft, 8 August 1990, Midale.

Carl and Margaret Hauglum interviewed by Michael Taft, 12 July 1990, Midale.

Marceline Lajimodiere interviewed by Olga Klimko, 17 July 1988, Estevan.

Arnold and Hazel Molstad interviewed by Michael Taft, 26 June 1990, Outram.

Jack and Joyce Muirhead interviewed by Michael Taft, 25 July 1990, Estevan.

Gerald, Margaret, and Wayne Pick interviewed by Michael Taft, 11 July 1990, Estevan.

Edgar Sawyer interviewed by Michael Taft, 26 June 1990, Macoun.

Clara Ziehl interviewed by Olga Klimko, 25 July 1988, Midale.

*In the Hanna family, there are two Ernies. The elder is usually called Uncle Ernie or "Big" Ernie. His nephew, whom we also interviewed, is sometimes called "Little" Ernie to distinguish him from his uncle.

References

Although we consulted several Souris Valley local history books and other printed sources, we took stories from the following two books only:

Gerald Boyer and Dwayne Boyer, compilers. *Memories*. Self-published by the Boyer Family, 1981.

Joan Gallaway. *Recollections of the Past*. Self-published by the author, 1974.

About the Authors

Olga Klimko has worked as an archaeologist for organizations such as the Saskatchewan Museum of Natural History and the Saskatchewan Research Council. She is a partner in Western Heritage Services, Inc., a private heritage consulting company based in Saskatoon.

Michael Taft is a folklorist who has worked in many areas of Canada. He is currently an associate of Western Heritage Services, Inc., and an adjunct professor of Anthropology and Archaeology at the University of Saskatchewan.